THE
HEART
OF THE
GREAT MOTHER

"*The Heart of the Great Mother* engages us in the most exciting possibilities to embrace all aspects of the feminine! Christine Page presents positive challenges to conventional doubts about the future."

C. NORMAN SHEALY, M.D., PH.D., PRESIDENT OF SHEALY-SORIN
WELLNESS AND HOLOS ENERGY MEDICINE EDUCATION
AND AUTHOR OF *BLUEPRINT FOR HOLISTIC HEALING* AND *LIVING BLISS*

"Christine Page is a remarkable wisdom keeper, and her book is a masterful and enlightening synthesis of ageless wisdom that speaks to our troubled times."

BRIAN LUKE SEAWARD, PH.D., AUTHOR OF *STAND LIKE MOUNTAIN,*
FLOW LIKE WATER: REFLECTIONS ON STRESS AND HUMAN SPIRITUALITY

PRAISE FOR PREVIOUS EDITION

"This is a magnificent book! Bravo, Dr. Page, for pulling all these sacred threads together in one place in this time of reawakening!"

CHRISTIANE NORTHRUP, M.D., AUTHOR OF *WOMEN'S BODIES,*
WOMEN'S WISDOM AND *THE WISDOM OF MENOPAUSE*

"Showing that a woman's purpose is to give birth not only to new life but also to new levels of consciousness, this book is a wake-up call for both humanity and every woman on the planet. I love this book."

DONNA EDEN, COAUTHOR OF *ENERGY MEDICINE*

"Christine R. Page, M.D., asks a question of timeless importance: 'How do we really connect with the feminine essence?' It's clear she has also lived the question, in both ordinary and extraordinary ways, making this more than an ordinary book, but a pure expression of the search for the most authentic answer. You'll discover insights and ancient wisdom on every page, because it is all within you, waiting for your inevitable embrace."

ANAIYA SOPHIA, AUTHOR *FIERCE FEMININE RISING*
AND *SACRED SEXUAL UNION*

"This book is filled with ancient wisdom that activates conscious awareness while simultaneously nourishing and renewing our souls."

LINDA STAR WOLF, FOUNDER OF VENUS RISING ASSOCIATION FOR TRANSFORMATION AND AUTHOR OF *SHAMANIC BREATHWORK*

"Filled with practical analogies, you will explore the depth of emotions and perceptions and learn to reconnect by examining the ancient, historic, and proven examples throughout the ages."

SONIA VON MATT STODDARD,
AWARENESS MAGAZINE, JANUARY 2013

"I found this book to be fascinating. As a woman, I appreciated her exploration into sacred feminine sexuality. . . . I rate this book Five Stars out of a Five Star rating and recommend that it be a part of any metaphysicians library."

KALA AMBROSE, *EXPLORE YOUR SPIRIT,* FEBRUARY 2013

"Throughout the book she ties it all to the physiology and function of the female body, asking women to begin honoring their bodies and themselves again. . . . this is a perfect follow-up to *Madly in Love with Me.*"

ANNA JEDRZIEWSKI, *RETAILING INSIGHT,* FEBRUARY 2013

"This book points out beautifully how the sacred feminine is intrinsically linked to conscious evolution. As a human race we have collectively gone unconscious and to wake up, women must dismantle old societal beliefs from the past. This is also a great read for men who are searching for their inner balance of masculine and feminine. This was a huge step for me to come into my own feminine power and to be a much-needed influence in the world around me."

DHARA LEMOS, *LOTUS GUIDE MAGAZINE,* APRIL 2013

"At this moment I urge you, courageous man or woman, to open your heart and spirit to investigate this book and find what wisdom awaits you, the deepest part of you, to help you answer an essential question, 'What am I here to do?' I believe this book helps provide an answer."

JEFF FERRANNINI, *PLANETARY SPIRIT,* JANUARY 2013

THE
HEART
OF THE
GREAT
MOTHER

Spiritual Initiation,
Creativity, and Rebirth

CHRISTINE R. PAGE, M.D.

Bear & Company
Rochester, Vermont

Bear & Company
One Park Street
Rochester, Vermont 05767
www.BearandCompanyBooks.com

Text stock is SFI certified

Bear & Company is a division of Inner Traditions International

First edition originally published in 2008 by Bear & Company under the title
2012 and the Galactic Center: The Return of the Great Mother
Second edition published in 2020 by Bear & Company under the title *The Heart
of the Great Mother: Spiritual Initiation, Creativity, and Rebirth*

Cataloging-in-Publication Data for this title is available from the Library of Congress

ISBN 978-1-59143-354-5 (print)
ISBN 978-1-59143-355-2 (ebook)

Printed and bound in the United States by Lake Book Manufacturing, Inc.
The text stock is SFI certified. The Sustainable Forestry Initiative® program
promotes sustainable forest management.

10 9 8 7 6 5 4 3 2 1

Text design by Priscilla H. Baker and layout by Virginia Scott Bowman
This book was typeset in Garamond Premier Pro and Gill Sans with Optima and
Perpetua used as display typefaces

To send correspondence to the author of this book, mail a first-class letter to the
author c/o Inner Traditions • Bear & Company, One Park Street, Rochester, VT
05767, and we will forward the communication, or contact the author directly at
www.christinepage.com.

❃

To the Great Mother who nurtures my soul

and

to my dear husband, Leland,

for his commitment to respect, honor, and

support my life's work

and

to love the goddess within me.

CONTENTS

PART THREE

The Twelve Stages of Evolution and Dissolution

INTRODUCTION

TEACHINGS BENEATH THE STARS

Once again I find myself kneeling in the warm sand, watching my beloved teacher whose face is lined and darkened by years of living in the harsh sun of the desert. It is all so familiar: the hot earth, the exquisite colors of the setting sun, and the trust I have in this man whose age is indeterminate but who carries an air both ancient and eternal.

Our stance is natural for nomadic people: one leg poised, ready to straighten and propel the body into flight at a moment's notice, and the other tucked under the body, allowing rest. It reminds me of the phrase *in the world but not of it*. At this moment my attention is focused on a fairly intricate mandala my teacher has been carefully sculpting in the sand for the past hour. He looks up, pleased with his efforts, and then without a word and with one swift move of his hand, he sweeps away the whole picture until all that is left is the smooth, virginal sand.

He smiles. "Remember that despite appearances, life is impermanent; here today, gone tomorrow. All dreams and ideas arise from a primal source, often described as the Great Mother or 'ocean of possibilities.' It is to here that all our creations will eventually return to enhance her collective consciousness. So what image of your future do you wish me to create for you now?" He has a glint in his eye, and his hand is poised over the sand, ready to draw.

"But change can't be that easy; you can't merely sweep your hand through the old and create something new," I say, amazed at the simplicity of this idea.

He smiles at my realization. "Of course it is; it has always been that simple. As a much-loved expression of the Great Mother, we are first and foremost creators and transformers of our reality. Unfortunately, many people fail to appreciate the extensive realm of possibilities readily available to them, preferring to live within the illusionary state of security offered by a familiar experience that has been well tried and tested, even though it brings them little pleasure or joy. Such individuals strive to rise above scarcity and into abundance without realizing that the poverty they wish to leave behind exists primarily within their own minds.

"Life has sadly become a struggle for so many people due to external circumstances. The fire of their free will has almost been extinguished, smothered by a belief that their life is controlled and fated by a higher authority or power and there is no escape. Yet the deep eternal fire of their soul cannot be extinguished. The intuitive heart is today sending out radiant pulses of light and love to help us remember that unlimited possibilities—associated with love, joy, and pleasure—are readily available to us *now!* This is not fantasy or wishful thinking; can you not feel the cells of the body starting to shimmer and feel excited once more? A deeply buried memory is starting to awaken, which, if nurtured with the help of the emotions, will create a fruitful future worthy of your soul's desires."

Satisfied with his demonstration, he settles back on his heel and continues: "The Earth and its inhabitants are presently engaged in a powerful time of transformation when the old paradigm is giving way to the new. In other words, we're dissolving to evolve.

"You are so lucky to be alive at this time! For, ever since the birth of a new twenty-six-thousand-year cycle on December 21, 2012, everybody is being given the opportunity to decide how future generations will live, for centuries ahead. But like my demonstration in the sand, before we can create a new image, we first need to release our attachment to the old pattern and bathe in the Great Mother's void or state of nothingness until we are filled with new inspiration. It's interesting, isn't it, that we use the same word (*inspiration*) for an in-breath as we do for receiving insights? You may be aware of what it feels like to hold your breath in at the height of inspiration, but try breathing out or expiring fully and then holding your breath."

As I do as I'm instructed, I feel a sense of deep peace descend over me as my busy thoughts fade into the distance. "This is the Great Mother's realm of creative potential," he continues, "where everything in your imagination is possible, just awaiting your personal touch to create definition. Holding your breath out for a few seconds may be relaxing, but living in the unknown or in an unformed state can be scary, especially when our security is so attached to what we know or believe about ourselves and the world.

"To many people, this transitional in-between time will appear unstructured and confusing, with the past practically complete and the future still to be born. And yet these extremely unique conditions that allow us to enter the mysterious realms of the Great Mother offer us the ultimate prize that all spiritual beings seek: the opportunity to know eternal life, to be free of karma, and to wield the wand of divine creation.

"For here, between the worlds, time collapses, space expands into infinity, and the veils between the dimensions drop, revealing a single feature: Now. Our challenge is to be able to release our obsessively emotional hold on the past and future so we can fully appreciate the rich choices the Great Mother is offering us at this time. Certain aspects are already in place, but the rest will depend on the energy and beliefs we take to the Great Mother's 'cookie shop of opportunities.' For if all you know are chocolate chip cookies, then that is all you'll look for in the cookie shop, completely ignoring the much wider selection."

"But why wouldn't everybody want to take advantage of this extraordinary time in our history?" I ask, bemused.

He leans forward again and draws some numbers in the sand:

40%   40%   15%   5%

"Despite the fact that all humans possess free will as their birthright and that many people feel their life today is a struggle and pray for change, when the sand is wiped clear and choice is offered, 40 percent of people will instantly recreate what has just been swept away. Another 40 percent, inadequately trained from youth to make their own decisions, will find the challenge of choice overwhelming and will instantly fall asleep, blank out, or lose themselves in menial mental tasks. Fifteen percent will become confused, which will be expressed as irritation, frustration, and disorientation, and 5 percent will understand. They will recognize the opportunity to be vanguards and light bearers of a new creative cycle, both for themselves and for the world in general.

"Let me be clear. It takes courage to enter the Great Mother's treasure trove; it's not just a matter of meditating or losing oneself in the realms of fantasy, because these are often associated with a structured process of 'doing' as well.

"Divine creation demands three qualities:

1. A willingness to dissolve into the love of the Great Mother
2. Right intention or purpose
3. Mastery of one's power

"It's common to think that we need to set intention first. Indeed, there's a plethora of courses teaching us 'how to create abundance, how to attract loving relationships, or how to have great sex' based on affirmations or prayers. But most of these methods rely on training the mind to think differently. Do you realize how hard that is? As Einstein indicated, we cannot solve our problems using the same level of thinking that created them.

"Your mind is trained to keep you perfectly safe by limiting any sudden changes or dangerous sojourns into unknown realms of consciousness and by creating beliefs, plans, and identities. As long as you hold strong beliefs such as 'The world is . . . , I am . . . , My plan is to . . . , People can't . . . ,' you think you are safe. The mind is like a computer; its knowledge is programmed by past experiences and/or ancestral beliefs. It is practically impossible to evolve as a spiritual human being by *only* following your mind. You have to learn to listen to your heart, which speaks to you through intuition and the power of love, urging you to enter the mystery of the unknown.

"The question to ask yourself is 'Do I believe deep down that I am loved?'

"This is the reason the first quality—the willingness to dissolve into the love of the Great Mother—is so important and yet the hardest to develop. We often cling desperately to our well-developed little ego or self-identity, as it provides security, despite inner feelings of stagnation and depression. But remember, we are cyclical beings; like the setting sun or the waxing moon, we need to dissolve back into the loving embrace of the Great Mother in order to evolve spiritually. It is only within her ocean of possibilities that we can gain access to an abundance of dreams or seeds of inspiration that await our attention. So first, we need to re-enforce, through our hearts, her eternal love for us. This is an ongoing process.

"In setting our intention it's important to recognize the different phases of our cyclical or, more accurately, spiraling nature. There is a phase of inspiration when seeds or new ideas are planted and nurtured. This is followed by the full expression or manifestation of the potential of that seed into the world, similar to a flower in full bloom. The idea has taken form and become matter and it's time to celebrate. The last phase sees dissolution of the form, when the wisdom or energy of the fruit is fed back into the original plant to make it stronger, allowing the bloom to die.

"Creation equates to cycles of birth, growth, nurturance, celebration, dissolution, death, and rebirth, each cycle spiraling toward the center without an end; immortality. Creation involves spirit moving into matter and matter back into spirit. *We need to make it matter before we realize it doesn't matter.* If you don't understand these phases, you may be trying to set an intention for growth when you really need to be allowing things to die.

"The last essential quality for divine creation is the mastery of our power. Where does this power come from? It derives from the development of our magician's wand that spirals up along our spine, stretching from beneath our feet to above our heads. During this transitional period we have the opportunity to tap into a force that has not been available to us for a long time. For now, all of our creations from other lives are returning to us so we can extract the light of consciousness—wisdom—from past stories or experiences and thus create a bright and powerful serpentine pillar of light, our wand.

"This is not a time to be limited by the fear of change or fear of the unknown re-enforced by a belief that somehow we don't deserve what the Great Mother has to offer. Why do you think there are so many souls on this planet at this time? For lifetimes everybody has been working toward this moment, determined not to allow this unique opportunity for soul transformation to pass them by, thereby forcing them to wait another twenty-six thousand years."

I let out a long, deep breath, for I know within my being the truth of what he is saying.

He smiles at my recognition. "The ancient Maya spoke of this era as a time when we enter a new world ruled by the element of ether, a world where there is a sacred marriage of opposites that will create a unified field of consciousness. This correlates to the fact that we're presently in the Piscean age, which began over two thousand years ago and will end around 2150 CE. The astrological symbol for Pisces is two fish swimming in opposite directions joined by a golden band, representing the sacred marriage of opposites, a phrase coined by Carl Jung. The message of this age is 'Love thy neighbor as thyself.'

"Very simple, you would have thought. But read any history book and it's clear we have done the exact opposite over the past two millennia. Even today we go to war against anybody who is not like us. It's time to wake up and behave responsibly, for we cannot evolve as a species until we release our emotional hold on all of our ridiculous prejudices and acknowledge the truth: Namaste; I am another one of you.

"Ether is considered to be the fifth element and the synthesis of the four other elements: earth, air, fire, and water.[1] According to the great mathematicians—the Pythagoreans—each element is represented by a different geometric form, together known as the platonic solids. They believed the constant movement and interrelationship between these elements, each of which can be expressed as a musical frequency, led to the formation of the galaxies and the universes and life as we know it.

"This new domain of ether is represented by unification, spaciousness, and invisibility, and is symbolized by the twelve-faced dodecahedron, which some say is the shape of the universe.[2] The number 12 is held in high regard by religious scholars and mystics. There were twelve tribes of Israel, twelve sons of Jacob, twelve fruits on the Tree of Life, twelve disciples of Jesus, twelve knights at Arthur's Round Table, and there are twelve signs of the zodiac.

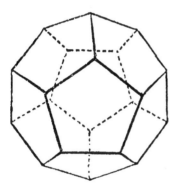

Figure I.1. The dodecahedron—one of the five platonic solids with its twelve faces
Illustration from 1908 *Chambers's Twentieth Century Dictionary of the English Language* by Reverend Thomas Davidson

"Each time the number is used, we are reminded of the twelve attributes that must be awakened within the human soul before we can gain access to the thirteenth dimension or realm of universal awareness, or what some call 'heaven.' I think you have met this shape before?" he asks.

Indeed I had! While exploring the complexity of what we perceive as reality, I learned that the Earth, similar to every human being, possesses an aura consisting of subtle energy bodies or grids of vibratory energy. Each grid is shaped like one of the platonic solids and fits neatly inside another grid, kept alive by different frequencies of consciousness, including our thoughts, feelings, and insights. As any one grid receives more attention and hence power from our collective consciousness, it emits a holographic image, which we then consider to be our reality. Hence, when the majority of the population expresses joy, we create and see the world as joyful. When fear is the primary emotion, the world becomes a place of secrets and anxiety exacerbated by our survival responses.

Over time we have forgotten the illusionary nature of reality—a collection of holographic images created by our own subconscious thoughts and emotions—causing us to believe the structure of our world is solid and cannot be changed. Yet, in essence, these loose collections of vibrating energies are capable of transforming themselves as quickly as it takes for us to change our mind!

For thousands of years, the main driving forces behind the creation of reality have been our emotions—linked to the element of water—and our beliefs or reason, represented by the element of air. Now, at the dawning of the new age of compassion, harmony, and interrelatedness, we are reconnecting to the soul grid that has been patiently waiting for our remembering. Taking the shape of a dodecahedron and represented by ether, it is known as the unity or Christ grid. "Am I right in thinking," I ask, "that Christ or unity consciousness has existed on this planet for a long time, even before the messiah Jesus, or Yeshua, walked upon the Earth? And is it also true that Christ consciousness is now becoming available to every human being as each of us strives to become whole or one with our soul's essence?"

He nods as I start to see how everything ties together. Then he continues: "Ether is celestial and lacks material substance, yet it is no less real than wood, wind, flame, stone, or flesh.[3] Within the context of ether there can be a fusion of polarities without the need for separation into darkness and light, negative and positive, good and bad, or even spirit and matter: unity through the loving acceptance of diversity. Everything is acknowledged as just another expression of the same divine essence, which begins with the Great Mother's loving gift of powerful creative potential."

His statement, unity through diversity, brings to mind the desire by some people in society today who wish to negate differences between people in the mistaken belief this will bring harmony. For instance, I'm often asked why I focus specifically on women's health and empowerment when surely men and women are essentially the same? I have to remind them there are major anatomical and physiological differences that allow the contributions to society by the different genders to be both unique and complementary. For thousands of years, cultures thrived because of their understanding that multiplicity brings the greatest degree of creative productivity. Indeed, it is well-known that when the gene pool becomes limited through lack of foreign integration, mental and physical illnesses increase, often leading to the extinction of such isolated civilizations.

Nature thrives on diversity and on the sacred marriage of opposites.

He continues: "As the poles of existence start to fuse and the veils between the dimensions dissolve, we will find ourselves becoming increasingly sensitive to the effect of our actions on others.[4] In other words, through our hearts we will feel what others feel without the luxury of guilt, blame, denial, and projection. In this way we will experience the true meaning of a sentiment found in many religions, including Buddhism, which states: 'Hurt not others in ways that you yourself would find hurtful, for you and I are one.'

"Imagine a world where denial of our interrelatedness is no longer an option. Imagine how a decision to injure or abuse others, whether physically or emotionally, would alter if we knew their pain would be our pain. When you and I are one, all feelings are shared, and instinctively we will select those actions that bring the greatest degree of harmony and joy. In essence, the world of ether presents us with the possibility of a peace upon this planet that truly surpasses our present-day understanding."

We look out across the desert as each of us reflects on a world where true harmonic unification occurs through the acceptance and celebration of our differences.

He resumes: "There are, of course, some who strive to maintain polarization, encouraging the enmity that exists between different factions, religions, political parties, and even sporting teams, secretly knowing this feeds their own selfish needs. They use fear, shame, and suspicion of each other to keep people separate, knowing that cooperation, compassion, and trust would lead to a disintegration of their tenuous authority. They are masters of charmed threats, which emotionally persuade others not to rock the boat and cleverly distort the true meaning of unity by saying 'my way or the highway.'

"To perpetuate their own cause, these societies or individuals often exploit the chaos and uncertainty that commonly exists during such transitional periods in our history. Such puppeteers frequently persuade their followers that they will only feel safe against the 'enemy' by returning to the old ways, controlled by them." It is not hard for me to identify present-day individuals or groups who have a vested interest in maintaining control through the incitement of fear and shame.

"Yet despite the propaganda," he continues, "large numbers of ordinary people are awakening to the fact that many of the dogmas that have been taught for centuries are based on flawed reasoning. Millions of people are beginning to listen to their own inherent guidance or intuition, which tells a very different tale. Through inner knowing they are reconnecting to the pulse of the Great Mother's heart and remembering that their soul's purpose or destiny in this life is to bring heaven onto earth to plant their unique seeds of consciousness and hence create a new world.

"Even those who appear preoccupied with emotions from the past or fear of the future are not immune to the Great Mother's call. Their cellular intelligence is listening, and the truth once heard is never lost.

"During the decades to come there will be a great need for all who consciously hear the call to encourage others to remember their inherent destiny. Together we can birth a world that encompasses the principles of cooperation and oneness through the acceptance of diversity, ensuring right relationship with all life-forms who share this planet."

He pauses to allow me to appreciate both the challenges and joys that lie ahead and then he looks out into the endless sky. "For those ancient people who believed their existence stretched beyond the confines of the Earth plane, the Milky Way was seen as the source of all Creation," he continues. "For some cultures it was known as the Great Mother, her

heart located at the center, the expansive white area of stars symbolizing her pregnant womb and the Dark Rift—a dark cleft of stardust—
representing her birth cleft or vagina.[5]

"For others, our galaxy was a great serpent, its gaping mouth represented by the Dark Rift dividing the white river of stars.[6] Whatever the
culture or analogy, the story was the same. It is from the Milky Way we
are born and nurtured, and it is to there we will return to die."

Figure I.2. The Milky Way as the Great Mother
Image by Dave Young, from flikr under the license CC BY 2.0

He stops while we both turn to honor the passing of the sun as
it dips beneath the horizon for another day. "The Maya kings under-
went shamanic journeys in service to their people, often taking on the
form of a powerful animal such as a jaguar," he continues. "Through
ritualistic practices they entered the serpent's mouth—the portal to the
underworld—and traveled through the darkness until they reached the
eternal source of all Creation.[7] Having immersed themselves in this
ocean of possibilities—the consciousness of the Great Mother—they
were reborn from the same orifice, bringing wisdom and inspiration to

their followers. As you can imagine, the ability of these shamanic leaders to move and commune between the worlds ensured the continuation of their powerful position within society.

"What is important for you to understand is that rather than merely sharing the words of their experience, they embodied this energy, thereby acting as a lightning rod or conduit for these new ideas or seeds of consciousness to be brought into the Earth. They were magicians and alchemists who could transform into matter the archetypal frequencies of energy that they had absorbed during their journey through the Galactic Center. They knew the secret of immortality. On many occasions, these alchemists would use stories, song, or poetry to express an idea or they would create art forms using geometric shapes to influence the consciousness, and hence destiny, of their people."

As he talks about the power of geometric patterns to inspire consciousness, I find myself picturing the thousands of crop formations that have appeared around the world since the late 1980s, the dates correlating with the acceleration of access to the Great Mother's treasure trove. These complex geometric designs (an example of which is shown in figure I.3) have been variously credited to the brilliance of extraterrestrials, the influx of sound waves, the power of the collective unconscious, and more recently to circle makers, a group of highly skilled human crop artists.

Whatever the source, these formations are known to carry specific vibrations of energy that marinate us in detailed archetypal patterns, influencing us on a profoundly cellular level. If string theorists are correct and consciousness consists of waves of varying frequencies impacting every moment of our lives,[8] then these universal shapes are, like a mold, forming and defining our thoughts and consequently our actions. In other words, they are determining the actualization of our world.

Although archetypal patterns impact us all, the final product is totally unique, influenced by the distinctive nature of our soul, expressing the perfection behind the universal plan. I look down at the grains of sand around my feet and marvel at how each is intricately different

Figure I.3. Crop formation in Switzerland, July 29, 2007

from the others, honed by the wind and the sun over the years, and each as beautiful as the next.

My dear friend, acknowledging the insights I have just received, continues: "The Great Mother's ocean of possibilities has been visited by many seers, yogi, and shamans throughout history, traveling along streams of projected consciousness. They describe dimensions ungoverned by the three-dimensional time-space paradigm, where there is access to multidimensional and parallel universes and where the source of all life exists. It has been called heaven, nothingness, zero point, and the void, although it is in no way empty but is instead full of potentiality. A more accurate term would be the *quantum plenum.*"[9]

My thoughts return to a recent lecture I heard on nonlocality and its inherent quality of interconnectedness. The speaker called this nonlocalized place *phase space,* a mathematical term that describes an invisible location consisting of vibrating fields of probability where every possible past and future is readily available—in other words, the Great Mother. Within this space there is no form or structure; everything exists as pure light or essential consciousness, which cannot be measured. All we can do is be present to its uncertainty. As soon as observation, attention, or analysis is applied, the wave form collapses, probability is changed into actuality, and particles of manifested reality are produced.

What I gleaned from this stimulating discussion is that it is only from a linear standpoint that we perceive a clearly defined past, present, and future. In this space of nonlocal reality, however, everything occurs in a state of dynamic suspended animation. What we call the past, present, or future are just different views of our holographic reality, brought into manifestation by simply changing the focus of our attention or angle of perception. When viewed in this way it's easy to appreciate the possibility of altering not only the future but also the past.

Excited by the links my mind is making, I look directly at my teacher and say, "As you describe the journey of sages, shamans, and kings to and from the Great Mother, my understanding of the mysteries of immortality is deepening. I now understand that in any moment I am immersed in eternal possibilities. As soon as I choose to pay attention to any one possibility, then it immediately shifts from being an energetic wave form to a finite particle; it becomes my reality. If I change my focus, the old focus of my attention transforms, once again becoming a wave form, and dissolves back into the ocean of possibilities enriched by its interactions with me. My new focus of attention is converted simultaneously from a wave of probability into a manifested form."

I laugh. "I counsel so many people who want to make changes in their lives, but at the same time I often hear them say, 'It's so difficult, it's going to take time.' I'm now going to say, 'It can happen in the blink of an eye. All you have to do is believe in this new reality, release your hold on the old holographic form, and become the change you want to bring to your world.'"

Delighted by my understanding, my teacher shifts his position in the sand. "There is a saying that is often misquoted: 'As above, so below.' To an alchemist the true message is 'As below, so above; as above, so below.'[10]

"Life is a continuum, represented by the serpent that eats its own tail, the Ouroboros, reminding us of the continual cycles of death and rebirth that occur time and again until there is only now. In terms of immortality, we see the creative source—the ocean of possibilities—and the creation—manifested reality—as equally honored, interchangeable, and essential to each other. In other words, spirit and matter are just different faces of the Divine. Each gives birth continually to the other at the expense of its own existence.

Figure I.4. The Ouroboros, which reveals the cyclic nature of our existence
Ouroboros, 1478 drawing by Theodoros Pelecanos, in the alchemical tract entitled *Synosius*

"The ability to shift frequencies between the vibration of spirit and the vibration of matter is possible because of the existence of a transformer found, not only within every human being, but also within the center of our sun and of our galaxy. This unique piece of equipment is the heart. Without it our very purpose as creative beings would grind to a halt as we're forced either to live a life of continual unrealized potential or to stagnate, paralyzed by the weight of our own creations. Can you now see why limiting thoughts and lack of joy are found to be major factors in the formation of heart disease? When we are disconnected from the spiritual pulse of our heart—intuitive knowing—we forget that we are immortal magicians and readily relinquish our wand of power to those who do not deserve it. It is now time to 're-member' who we are; it's time to listen to the call of the heart.

"In more modern terms, this miraculous heart could be called a star gate, transporting us naturally between the many different dimensions. Anybody who has ever been in love knows of the heart's capacity for transformation. Held within the energetic embrace of your lover, time dissolves, space expands, and anything is possible. Everybody you encounter within this blissful existence appears loving, beautiful, and without a flaw. Here you experience the essential quality of spiritual existence, and it feels wonderful. Now the challenge is to create such a heartfelt space wherever you go, mirroring the energy that radiates from the heart of the Great Mother; the energy we call love.

"In order to embody such a state of immortal freedom, we must first build and then increasingly occupy our light body or Ka, the vehicle that allows us to escape the confines of time and space."

The mention of the Ka reminds me of Tom Kenyon and his book the *Magdalen Manuscript*,[11] in which he describes the alchemical teachings of the Egyptians in their quest for immortality. They understood that each of us has three bodies: the Khat or physical body, the Ka or light body, and the Ba or higher self. Through deep inner work and alchemical practices, they aspired to activate each of the body's chakras, thereby sending serpentine energy up a central connecting pathway, the Djed, which is positioned along the spine. The process, known as the *raising of the Djed,* is clearly synonymous with the raising of the dead, or the transformation of base consciousness into the golden consciousness of enlightenment. It is also the reason why the sacred heroes in the *Star Wars* stories are called Jedi knights, implying they are alchemists who have mastery of their Djed, or serpentine sexual fire.

In order to reach immortality, it was taught that there must be an alignment between the energy within the Djed and the Ba, the higher or spirit self. When this sacred marriage occurs, there is an influx of energy into the Ka, igniting it to produce a golden raiment or cloak. The immortal body has thus been created.

My desert teacher, conscious of my understanding, takes up the thread. "Such a process toward immortality often takes many lifetimes. Yet at this moment in our history it is within the reach of all dedicated students of alchemy as long as they remember the warning given by the great alchemist St. Germain, who said, 'Any developing alchemist must guard against self-delusion and rationalization.'[12]

"There are also specific instructions that are essential to the development of the Ka or light body. These include:

- Be present in the now, without attachment to the past and future.
- Know that reality is created through focused attention.
- Apply full power and intention until our dreams are transformed into matter, and then realize it doesn't matter!
- Be accountable and compassionate for all of our creations.
- Have an understanding that it is through our creations, whether these are enjoyable events, challenging situations, or our relationships, that our consciousness grows."

I'm taken back to a time when I communicated with the Sleeping Lady of Malta, an archetypal facet of the Great Mother. I asked her why it was that humanity did not have full access to the multidimensional realms, despite our apparent advances in science. She was very clear: "Eighteen thousand years ago, humankind was able to traverse the portals between the worlds and enjoy the rich source of creative potential. But sadly, two things occurred, which highlighted humanity's spiritual immaturity. First, most were unwilling to be accountable for their creations, especially those they considered unacceptable. Second, they tried to personally possess those things that did not belong to them. From that moment on, humanity was blocked from accessing these higher realms until now."

I'm reminded of the words of another wise friend: "Karma is taking something that doesn't belong to you." It feels good that we're being given a chance to change our ways, although I'm not convinced we've made many advances when it comes to spiritual maturity, given that greed, nonaccountability, and corruption are all too evident in many areas of society today.

I return from my reverie and my nomadic teacher continues. "The masters of the Great Work of alchemy describe the twelve stages of the development of the Ka in terms of cycles of inspiration and expiration. The phases of inspiration that lead to manifestation of form are similar to the expanding or waxing light of the moon, from the new moon to the full moon. During this phase we are asked to:

- Listen to our intuition or inner wisdom
- Nurture and support our dreams and ideas
- Own our power, both physical and spiritual
- Accept the dual nature of existence and face the mirrors of our dispossessed self
- Bring any dream into manifestation and celebrate

"These phases of inspiration involve the growth and development of the 'ego-hero' who journeys until his dreams are fully realized and he becomes king or sovereign of his own creations.

"But this is only half of the cycle and, on expiration—similar to the waning moon—the ego-king must prepare to die, offering back to the ever-expanding Great Mother the wisdom of his earthly experiences so she in turn can give birth to the new sun or ego, ensuring that the cycle continues.

"Thus the stages of expiration require us to:

- Enhance the process of contemplation and introspection
- Strengthen the power of self-love to ensure we turn away from the outer world and back toward our core
- Descend into the boiling cauldron of the Dark Goddess, where the meat of our 'stories' are dissolved until only the bones remain
- Meet those aspects of the self that became separated through shame and fear and accept them into the heart without judgment
- Transform the physical form into spiritual essence
- Complete the development of the magician's wand or Djed, through which we can reach the Ba
- Experience the sacred marriage, flow into our Ka, and merge with the immortal heart of the Great Mother"

He waits as the impact of his words fully pervades my awareness. Deep within my heart I know what he says is true and yet at the same time I'm surprised to feel a few nagging concerns arising, demanding to be heard: "What if I miss the boat? What if I get it wrong?"

He laughs at my honesty. "See how quickly your limiting and unre-solved fears override the sense of knowing and excitement? This is nor-mal and helps you to recognize those parts of your consciousness that have become separated over time and await integration. For example, remember an idea or dream that so excited you that you couldn't wait to bring it into form and make it reality? Then remember what happened when the manifested dream was not as you imagined it would be. You felt disappointed and probably quickly found ways to distance yourself from this unacceptable creation and move on to something new.

"Yet in doing this, you abandoned a part of your soul's conscious-ness, for this is the basis of any idea or dream. By rejecting or failing to be accountable for this piece of your manifested creation, one aspect of your wholeness remains closed and separate from you. It is inherent in you to return and courageously tear away the outer coverings of the 'story'—old emotions and beliefs—until you can glean the gems of wis-dom (knowledge in action) waiting within.

"This is much easier when we stop seeing ourselves as victims of our own life and begin to know ourselves as its creator. Believe me, every-body is a mighty soul who created their life with all of its challenges so they could know wholeness. Life is a complex business and it's not always apparent at first why anyone would have chosen to experience pain, suffering, or loss. That is why self-reflection and detachment are so important for soul growth, especially when viewing events from the past. Begin your inquiry with: 'Knowing that I am a mighty creative being, how has my inner light expanded due to that particular situation or crisis in my life? What gems of wisdom can I take from that event?' Unless we have the courage to look within, shedding the veil of victim-hood, we will never gather enough strength to build our light body and hence we will never know the joy of becoming cocreators of the new world that we are destined to become.

"The Dark Goddess—part of the trinity that makes up the Great Mother—is in residence now, inviting us to enter her fiery cauldron so that we may recover gems of wisdom from all of our creations over the past twenty-six thousand years and hence experience or know ourselves fully. As we gather the wisdom, our light of consciousness increases until we are able to fully inhabit our Ka body."

"What happens to the parts of me I choose to ignore?" I ask.

He answers without hesitation. "This is a time to complete karma and extricate yourself from the many illusions you have developed about yourself and the world in general. Any subpersonalities or archetypal complexes that you do not possess will possess you, becoming the originating source of your creations over and over again, until you take notice. This is not a form of punishment as some would like to believe, saying, 'This always happens to me,' but instead is a gift, reinforcing the impetus to embody our soul's incarnation. Useful questions to ask are: 'What patterns of experiences keep repeating themselves in my life? What do I judge in others that may be reflecting a part of me that I'm trying to ignore?' Remember, when you experience a heightened emotional response to someone you meet, they are showing you a part of yourself that is awaiting integration. Whether you feel happy, irritated, envy, or fear around someone, ask yourself: What am I meeting in this person that's still waiting in the shadows of my own psyche?

"The Dark Goddess or Crone doesn't have a good reputation; she often trails confusion, death, and destruction in her wake. Yet during this transformative process, her love for us is stronger than ever. She knows that in order for a new world to be born, the old must be allowed to die. Even now, her vulture-like nature is tearing away the meat from our old, redundant stories until only the bones of our essential consciousness remain."

With his words I can sense her presence physically, and it feels remarkably reassuring.

"So what you're saying is the more I call home those parts of me that have become separated, for whatever reason, and find a way to accept their presence in my life, the more energized my light body will be and the greater the chance I'll have to embrace my dreams for the future?"

In an instant I realize there will be no need for a messiah or guru to lead us. *We* are the ones we have been waiting for! It is our combined consciousness, the very thoughts I am entertaining at this moment, which will shape our destiny. Through this portal of opportunity we are being handed the keys to the doors of heaven so we can bring cosmic riches down to the Earth. Then a thought crosses my mind: What would have been the reaction of the king-shamans or priests of the past if their sacred position in society was challenged by the ability of their subjects to make the same journey and speak directly to the source? It would perhaps beg the question, "Why do we need a king?"

We are truly entering a time of personal empowerment, when self-consciousness and respect for the unique contributions of every individual—symbolizing the forthcoming Aquarian age—is superseding the old Piscean model in which an individual's existence is dependent on the beliefs and dogmas of an elite few.

It suddenly dawns on me that an extremely clever plan has been set in place to be activated at this time. Each soul has been given a unique piece of the jigsaw puzzle that, when brought together with all the other parts, will create the fullness of our future. Yet in order for this to happen, we as a species must learn to work together, valuing and encouraging the contributions of every individual; no one piece is more important than another. I see this concept as a true reflection of the ideals of the world of ether, where all aspects are equally accepted and loved by the Great Mother.

My teacher's words make me realize we're all being offered the chance to become fully realized spiritual human beings. "But why wouldn't everyone want to strive for such joyful perfection?" I ask him. He replies with a sigh. "When you have forgotten the sweet embrace of the immortal self, you will cling to your possessions—material, emotional, or mental—as lifelines, even though these attachments have long since failed to nurture your soul, appeasing only the small ego or personality. It's so hard to appreciate that these changes aren't happening to you—but are mainly being directed *by* you, immersed as you are in a mythology that a higher power directs your every move. It is the ego that maintains the separation, the soul that knows the truth, and the Great Mother who calls us home."

He looks out as the dying sun's rays set the sky on fire, an omen for the times ahead. "I don't deny there are challenges before us as we begin our journey back to the embrace of the Great Mother. But as long as we listen to our hearts the truth is clear: It is time to dissolve back into the ocean of possibilities so that we may cast our line afresh and bring forth a golden age of unity and peace.

"The ancient people knew this time would come and left encrypted messages for us to find. These were hidden within mythological tales, ancient songs, poetry, art, and sacred sites, especially those that employ sacred geometry. Today we are seeing a revival of interest in all things sacred and mysterious, with even the scientific world dedicating serious research time and money to the study."

He looks down at the sand he recently cleared. "I took great pride in creating my beautiful picture, and yet that same pride should not prevent me from allowing each grain of sand to return to its source. Nothing is permanent. The dissolution of our present state of consciousness has already started. It is mirrored by events around the world, both natural and man-made, causing us to release unhealthy attachments to the old ways and embrace the spirit of cooperation and compassion.

"Watch the birds and other winged animals—including the dolphins, which are the birds of the ocean—for unlike the four-legged, they are not tied to the Earth. They are forming closer and closer ties to the human race, communicating directly with our spirits and urging us to stretch our ethereal wings and rise above any delusion of limitation."

My awareness drifts to thoughts of my beautiful garden, which is commonly visited by hummingbirds, blue jays, and finches. In the skies above hawks glide in the warm thermals. My eyes meet those of my companion, and any separation between our souls disappears in waves of joy.

"The journey to the new world is through every heart," he says, "whether found in the center of the galaxy, the center of the sun, the nucleus of a cell, the body of a curious and adventurous child, or within the breast of your joyful hummingbird. Remember to celebrate every moment, take nothing for granted, and let your inner wisdom be your guide."

His final words are almost lost as I feel myself being bathed in an overwhelming wave of love, which seems to be simultaneously emanating from and flowing into my heart. Everything seems perfectly clear, and for once my head isn't directly involved.

"Seek out the knowledge of previous episodes of great change that took place on this planet, often hidden in your mythology," he advises. "To the uninitiated, these cultural tales are merely stories told to children and yet they were designed poetically by your predecessors to awaken your dormant memory when the time is right. Now is that time. The symbols contained within these tales resonate with your eternal mind, reminding you of a truth that is beyond the understanding of the logical mind. While the intellect will look for a list of things to do, the heart will be fed by all the love and wisdom it needs. Each cultural myth carries archetypal frequencies of consciousness embodied within the lives of that particular culture's gods and goddesses. When shared, these powerful vibrations stir the smoldering embers of our soul, and we remember.

"At the same time, study the craft of alchemy, the science of the mystics, for these great scientists knew how to turn the base consciousness of ignorance into the golden consciousness of enlightenment and immortality."

He stands slowly, and I know our time together is coming to a close. He adds, "This is the moment you've been waiting for. It's hard for you and others to appreciate the amount of preparation you undertook to be ready for this particular incarnation. You will meet many others who signed up for this great adventure; together you will act as conduits to bring a new frequency of consciousness to this planet."

And with that, the vivid scene disappears and I emerge from a deep meditation. On opening my eyes, I see the Milky Way snaking its way across the night sky high above the Big Island of Hawaii. In that moment, I know my life has changed forever.

This meeting in the desert took place some years ago. In retrospect, I had few clues then as to where to begin my search for archetypal patterns of transformation but, as always happens in my life, the areas to explore began to emerge spontaneously, allowing the pieces to fall naturally into place. I began avidly to search for mythological stories that could provide me with clues as to how the ancient people dealt with the challenges and chaos that often seem to accompany times of global transformation. As my study of mythology deepened, it became clear that much of the instructive wisdom, cleverly encoded into ancient tales, not only teaches us how to surf the waves of change but also how to embrace the same eternal existence as the gods and goddesses of old. For instance, some of their stories contain specific details about the extraction of the elixir of life or the ambrosia of the gods that is essential for the attainment of immortality.

I also came to see that a lifetime of involvement in metaphysical studies had not been wasted as the most enduring systems of esoteric knowledge such as tarot, astrology, numerology, and alchemy all contain within them detailed instructions of the steps required to be taken by the diligent initiate to find their way into the heart of the Great Mother.

Yet through my studies, I have also discovered that, as with all good secrets, the path is closely guarded and accessible only to those who journey with purity of heart, mastery of their desires, and detachment from the result. This is underscored by the following warning from the Mayan wisdom text, the Popul Vuh: "The Truth is Hidden from the Seeker and Searcher."[13] The same sentiment is found in this text from the Gospel of Thomas: "The Knowledge has been hidden from those who wish to enter . . . Be as innocent as doves and as wise as serpents."[14]

When I first read these words, I was reminded that despite my many inept attempts to plan my future, things often work out much better when I step back and trust! For example, about ten years before my desert meditation, I became fascinated by all things Mayan. I traveled the Ruta Maya, studied the Mayan calendar, and ensconced myself in the secrets of the crystal skulls, which are commonly associated with these ancient people. It was during my travels that I just happened to meet a man in a remote area of Belize. Over numerous cups of coffee,

I was enthralled by his stories encapsulating the mysteries surrounding the ancient Maya.

Certain descriptions remain in my mind even today: The Maya are masters of illusion, keepers of the portals to the holographic universe. In the ancient past they set time-space locks on these portals or doors so they could be opened only by those whose level of consciousness ensured that what lay beyond would be used with wisdom and respect. What archaeologists and the media call a "discovery" is merely the opening of a portal that occurs when humankind's awareness reaches a level of consciousness that then allows a certain holographic energetic blueprint to manifest into a solid form.

The Maya also hid their precious artifacts in areas that even today are easily overlooked as insignificant, such as within a piece of unculti-vated land. At the same time, they marked doorways into their mystical world by leaving certain artifacts unfinished, broken, or out of place. Hence we see that despite the skills of the master craftsmen who built the magnificent tomb for Lord Pakal, in Palenque, Mexico, one corner of the lid of the lord's sarcophagus is damaged. To the Maya, there are no coincidences and everything has a purpose, offering us a focal point that leads us out of the three-dimensional world and into our multi-dimensional reality.

Such ancient stories about the Maya, inhabitants of this Earth long before their recent incarnation in 250–950 CE, are similar to myths from other cultures such as the Inca. I remember being told that the Inca wisdomkeepers predicted the arrival of the Spanish to their lands. Consequently, they hid everything that they considered valuable—especially their amazing golden discs—in the fourth dimension, unreach-able by their greedy invaders. But now in the past few decades, the Inca shamans feel it is safe to bring these precious objects back from their hid-ing place, into our three-dimensional world so they can be rediscovered!

Today, as I travel around the globe, I remember these teachings and recount many occasions when I'm intuitively led into the ancient mys-teries of a culture—not by following the tourist path or agreeing with an archaeologist's modern explanation, but by following my heart.

It is this light of wisdom that I offer to you with the hope of creating an energetic wormhole into the multidimensional nature of our existence. Come with me now as we attempt to open portals into the Great Mother's mysteries so we may see beyond the illusions and shadows and know ourselves fully as the brilliant and eternal light beings that we truly are.

PART ONE

From Creation to Immortality

It feels natural to begin our journey in the "place" from which everything is born and will eventually return. In our modern world, this is described as Light, God, the Source, or the Great Mother—an all-inclusive energy without differentiation. More scientific terms include the *holographic universe, phase space*, or *the void*, implying the energetic synthesis of all that has been and will ever be. We will explore all this and more in part 1 of this book.

1

THE TRIPLE GODDESS

Meeting the Great Mother

For the ancient people, including the Egyptians, Sumerians, and Babylonians, the origin of life was called the *primordial waters of nothingness,* possessing strong feminine characteristics such as darkness, chaos, and fiery creative power. In other words, in the beginning was powerful feminine potentiality, similar to the matrix, awaiting fertilization into form.

Such unlimited vastness is often difficult for our small minds to grasp, causing us to seek definition in terms of size and function and leading to our personalized view of God, complete with human opinions and biases. This propensity to see everything through our lens is the very reason why it is said that the name of God should not be spoken, for in doing so we limit its existence immediately. Similarly, our tendency to see everything from an objective viewpoint relative to ourselves causes us to externalize this encompassing energy and hence to perceive God as an entity separate from ourselves. In truth, we exist within this divine oneness, affecting and affected by everything that vibrates with the same spirit.

THE TRIPLE GODDESS

As we continue to explore the ancient Creation myths, we learn that from these primordial waters, the Great Mother gives birth to herself. This creates the Triple Goddess, consisting of the three archetypal faces of the feminine: Virgin, Mother, and Crone. Each face is essential for the complete creative process to transpire. Together they express the divine power of the Great Mother. The Virgin represents creative inspiration, the Mother creative nurturing, and the Crone creative transformation. All three of them act exclusively through their unique style of compassion and intuition, ever expanding our awareness of ourselves toward our perfect eternal state.

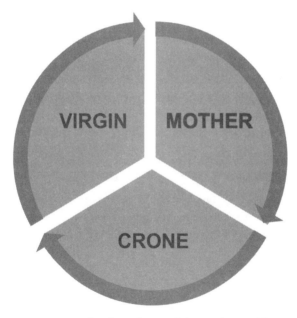

Figure 1.1. The three faces of the Triple Goddess,
revered from time immemorial

Representations of this Triple Goddess are found throughout traditional texts, appearing as Parvati-Durga-Uma (Kali) in the Hindu tradition; Anand-Badb-Macha or Eriu, Banba, and Fodla (the Morrigan) in Ireland; Hebe-Hera-Hecate in Greece; Guinevere in the Arthurian legend; the druidic Diana Triformis; and the Roman Fates.

Traditional wisdom tells us the Triple Goddess was honored as far back as 35,000 BCE. But in the past thirty-five hundred years, under patriarchal rule, the Goddess and everything associated with the feminine (intuition, emotions, and rhythmic cycles) have been suppressed or denigrated. Yet without the embodiment of these gifts of the Triple Goddess, whatever our gender, we will be unable to fulfill our soul's destiny.

Intuition maintains the connection to our soul's blueprint.

Emotions act as the force behind all creativity and transformation.

Cycles ensure evolution through transformation that occurs through inspired growth, embodiment of wisdom, and the release of old patterns or things that no longer serve us.

THE ONENESS IN EVERYTHING

The Mystical Yoni (Vulva)

One of the best-known symbols of the Triple Goddess is the oval-shaped yoni, or vulva, the name reminding us that we're in the presence of everything and nothing: the One. To the ancient people the vulva was sacred because, whether we emerge from it as a newborn baby or pass through it during the act of sex, it is an opening or portal into another dimension.

Unfortunately, as the honoring of the feminine faded so did our understanding of the role that the Triple Goddess plays in the sacred act of sexual intercourse. We have almost forgotten that it is the Virgin who excites us sensually, the Crone whose sexual fires burn away anything that keeps us separate from ourselves, and the Mother whose waves we blissfully play in at the height of our ecstasy.

During the past millennium, the mystical qualities of the yoni, or vulva, have been corrupted and almost lost, obscuring the door to our spiritual heritage. However, the Great Mother—as the Triple Goddess—has heard our cry and is returning to reclaim her children with a resurgence of interest in all things feminine, exemplified, for example, by the runaway success of Eve Ensler's *The Vagina Monologues.*[1]

The Vesica Piscis

The yoni is perfectly designed in the shape of a vesica piscis, formed when the circumference of one circle passes through the center of another, creating between them a two-pointed oval known as a portal into unity consciousness.

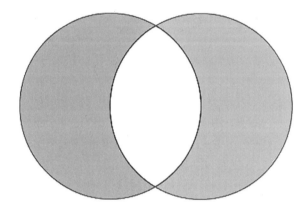

Figure 1.2. The vesica piscis, in which all three aspects
of the Triple Goddess are reflected

The circles themselves are seen to represent opposite poles of existence that come together while maintaining their own unique identity; attraction and repulsion creating unity through diversity. The willingness of the circles to unite in such an intimate way reminds us of how important it is to love and respect ourselves before we can truly develop right relationship with another person.

As the two circles come together to create the third inner shape, we see all three aspects of the Triple Goddess reflected. Together they give meaning to the saying "For where two or three are gathered together . . . there am I among them" (Matthew 18:20).* This simple message alludes to far more than the physical presence of a single person. It reveals that if we wish to know the oneness of eternal life—unity or Christ consciousness—we must first embody all three aspects of the Triple Goddess. At the same time, the complex nature of the forces involved in this sacred geometric pattern remind us that it is only through the harmonic interplay between repulsion and attraction, or light and dark, that the doorway into our multidimensional existence will become available to us.

THE GODDESS IN SACRED ARCHITECTURE

As we continue our exploration of the Triple Goddess it's fascinating to note there are many architectural representations of the yoni, although its identity—as the doorway or entrance into a place of oneness or wholeness with ourselves—has often been lost along with its significance.

From the twelfth through the fifteenth centuries, reverence of the Goddess was kept alive in the design of many of the great Gothic cathedrals of Europe, as we can see in figure 1.3. Representing the Mother Church, most were built with magnificent oval arched doorways symbolizing the yoni or vesica piscis, which led into the nave or womb of the church. Further back in time certain Greek temples—such as the Pantheon—were built around the geometry of the vesica piscis to heighten the reverence within. This geometry was reflected in the dimensions of the side walls of the temple, which were based on the ratio of 1 to the square root of 3. Perhaps the architects of these buildings wanted future generations to know that:

- It is through our inner feminine that we may reach the unified field of the kingdom of heaven.
- Unity consciousness is accessed through compassion and joy.
- The sacred geometry of these buildings emanates a frequency that

---

*All Bible quotes are based on the English Standard Version.

Figure 1.3. Gothic cathedral entrance,
a portal to the church proper

Engraving by E. Challis after a picture by T. Allom of the
entrance to Lincoln Cathedral in England, published 1837

allows us to be embraced by the unconditional love of the Great
Mother without the need for an intermediary.

It is clear that the present-day practices of certain religions have
strayed far from the conditions laid down by these medieval designers.
At the same time, many of today's architects still do not understand
how the vibrational qualities of sacred symbols influence the over-
all function of a building. Even when there is an acknowledgment of
the power of geometry to enhance our experience within a structure,
many modern buildings have no feminine curves. Instead they employ
straight lines that, rising skyward, exude masculine power.

Sheela-na-gigs

From the eleventh century onward, across Europe and especially in
Ireland and Britain, architects went even further to ensure that the
congregation honored the Divine Mother. This was accomplished by

Figure 1.4. Sheela-na-gig

carvings known as Sheela-na-gigs. These statues, often found in the walls or over the doorway of a church, depict naked females with full bellies posing in such a manner as to display and emphasize the genitalia. Many of them reveal a woman with her knees apart and the vesica-piscis-shaped hole of the vulva held open by one or both of her hands.

There are various accounts of the symbolic meaning of these images, including a particularly patriarchal view that maintains they were produced to protect men from eternal damnation by reminding them of the lustful nature of women. It is more likely, however, that they represented something far more significant than just a by-product of Christian dogma. The meaning of the word *Sheela-na-gig* is best translated as "vulva or spirit woman."

These figures closely resemble the yonic statues of Kali that appear at the doorways of many Hindu temples to confer good luck on all who enter. The protruding rib cage seen in several of the Irish carvings is also prominent in statues of Kalika, the death goddess of the Hindus. She is symbolized in Celtic tradition by Cailleach, the Crone or Hag, who is both the creator and the destroyer, and who appears younger as she passes from winter to spring. Thus the Sheela-na-gig is believed to represent all three aspects of the Goddess—Virgin (yoni), Mother (belly), and Crone (ribs)—the seasonal cycles of Mother Earth.

There is little doubt that the Celtic Christian Church in the first millennium was far more liberal and aware of the importance of the feminine within its society than its Roman counterpart. For example, it allowed divorce well into the twelfth century. Indeed, up until the ninth century "pagan" beliefs and sacred practices were openly accepted within a highly integrated religious discipline. Eventually the ancient Celtic contribution was suppressed and the Roman Catholic influence promoted these effigies as crude exhibitionist images. Yet it's interesting to note that the Sheela-na-gigs are reappearing all around Ireland and Britain as people seek out ways to commune with the energies of the Triple Goddess once more.

The Triangle

Another symbol commonly used to represent the yoni of the Triple Goddess is the triangle, located at the entrance of many sacred sites. The triangle is associated closely with the Oriental goddess Cunti, from whom are derived words such as *county, country, ken* (to know), *cunning,* and *cunt.* Clearly representing something different from modern-day usage, *cunt* is not a word of derision but one of respect, honoring the embodiment of the Goddess within a woman.

The same derivation gives us the word *kin,* or "family," leading to the word *kingdom,* which denotes "the domain of a king or queen." In olden days a kingdom was land that was passed down through a matrilineal pattern—mother to child—emphasizing the importance of the mother's bloodline. Indeed, in Ireland the land was seen as a sovereign queen that the king had to woo and be found acceptable by to earn his kingdom. Our ancestors knew that the continuation of a family and its fruitfulness on all levels was dependent on the mother and her link to the sovereign Mother Earth or goddess energy. Modern-day science reenforces this belief as we now know it is the mitochondrial genes that convey the strength to survive, and that a baby receives these genes only from its mother.

The Shamrock

There is another symbol found within the Celtic world that represents the Triple Goddess: a tiny, three-petal plant called the shamrock. Despite the fact that this national symbol of Ireland is usually associated with St. Patrick and his interpretation of the Trinity as Father, Son, and Holy Ghost, its importance stretches back far beyond his auspicious arrival on the Emerald Isle. It is now generally accepted that the myths around this patron saint of Ireland, who died in 496 CE, were written in the eighth century when a cult figure—holding a shamrock and killing snakes—was required to boost the supremacy of the church of Armagh in Ulster.

As so often happens when a new paradigm imposes itself onto a much older one, the personal details of actual historical figures are stolen or changed to create an entirely new persona that matches the dogma taught at the time. The original character is sold to the people as a fraud or a heathen and eventually becomes demoted in history into a mythical figure. Thus the pagan representative of Patrick was probably the Irish god of the shamrock, Trefuilngid Tre-eochair, who is said to have "controlled the rising and setting of the sun, carrying an immortal branch with flowers, fruit, nuts, apples and acorns all growing at the same time."[2] His consort was Macha, a sovereignty goddess of ancient Ireland and one of the faces of the Irish Triple Goddess, the Morrigan. Clearly the shamrock reflects the triple yoni of this Great Goddess, dating back to about 2500 BCE. This brings a whole new meaning to the wearing of the shamrock on St. Patrick's Day!

The Celtic Cross

The shamrock was probably the model for yet another important Celtic symbol reflecting the sun wheel, later modified into the present-day Celtic cross. With its three short arms and long vertical arm, the Celtic cross captures the image of the phallus held within the triple-faced yoni—the marriage of the male and female, the symbol of fertility and the continuation of life.

Indeed, the design of the most well-known monument in Ireland—Newgrange—is based on the principle of the Celtic cross. There, when

Figure 1.5. The Celtic cross

walking down a long passageway (the phallus), visitors enter a tall, round cavern from which three smaller openings (the Triple Goddess) emerge. For five days around the winter solstice, if the weather is clement, the rays of the sun enter a small box above the entrance and pass down the corridor, eventually penetrating the cavern and filling it with light.

To the mystic, this act symbolizes the fertilization, by a new spark of cosmic light, of Mother Earth's dormant eggs, so she can give birth to a whole new frequency of consciousness as the sun returns to the Northern Hemisphere. From the depths of Newgrange, the Mother nurtures the new baby until she deems it ready to leave the confines of its stone home. From there its unique message is spread throughout the globe via the Earth's complex grid system, so that all living things may be touched by its energy.

Sacred sites aligned to the solstices can be found all around the world. Like Newgrange, which is linked to the winter solstice, they highlight the Virgin's love in giving birth to and nurturing the boy-child until he leaves home as the hero. On the other hand, those sites that are linked to the summer solstice, such as Stonehenge, are connected to the Crone and the dying sun. This represents the beginning of the descent of the crowned king into the underworld where, six months later, he will eventually offer his life for the sake of his new son and heir. We will explore the journeys of the boy-child, hero, and king in more detail in later chapters.

The Spiral: A Representation of Ever-Present Change

In front of the entrance to Newgrange is a large oblong stone with intricate carvings displaying the three-spiraled head of the Celtic cross, reminding the visitor that this is the sacred domain of the Triple Goddess. The symbol of the spiral is found throughout the world, carved into the stone of many sacred sites. In most cultures the glyph depicts the great serpent mother who is said to have created the entire world from the place of formlessness. To the followers of Kali she is known as kundalini, whose curled up and unmanifested self is represented by a dot. The unfolding of this creative serpentine energy into form and its return into formlessness

Figure 1.6. The ancient monument of Newgrange, Ireland

is symbolized by the spiral, reminding the observer that the movement between form and formlessness is two-directional and continuous, and indeed, the very principle behind immortality.

The spiral is seen to be the most effective way of enhancing creative energy. The fact that the spirals found on the walls of the inner caverns of Newgrange are aligned with the lunar standstills reminds us of the powerful influence of the moon on our own creative cycles. These astronomical events are associated with maximum fertility of the mind, body, and spirit (which we will discuss in greater detail later).

The Natural Landscape of Glastonbury

In the ancient city of Glastonbury, England, the image of the Triple Goddess is revealed naturally in the landscape.[3] The gently rising Wearyall Hill is seen as one of her outstretched legs; the Chalice Well, her heart; and the famous tor, her head. This shimmering grassy hill, visible for miles around, contains the markings of a three-dimensional Cretan labyrinth, a sure sign that the tor was considered a sacred portal into the other or underworld, the very home of the Crone.

Beneath the Goddess's womb are the ruins of Glastonbury Abbey. With its straight lines and towers, its design contrasts starkly with the curves and flow of the surrounding landscape and reflects the patriarchal influence that was present in the thirteenth century during the abbey's construction. Yet beneath its main structure is a more ancient ruin known as the Mary or Lady Chapel. Dedicated to the womb of the Mother, it was built around the sacred geometry of the vesica piscis, representing creative unity.

The final representation of the Goddess in Glastonbury is marked by a small hill called St. Bride's Mound. It is found in Beckery, west of the main town. This simple rise in the landscape is seen to symbolize the head of the baby as it appears from the Virgin's yoni, or vulva. Metaphysically the mound also represents the head of the fully evolved hero-king who, as lover, willingly dives back into the vagina of the Crone to complete his journey.

Despite the fact that the land on which St. Bride's Mound stands is privately owned, not acknowledged as a sacred site, and is located behind a disused sewage works, it was once the gateway to the mysti-

Figure 1.7. The fascinating Glastonbury
Tor in Somerset, England

cal Isle of Avalon (Isle of Apples). This ancient location emanates an
ethereal energy where the veil between the worlds is thin and there is
easy access to the other dimensions. In the past, Avalon was indeed
an island, with waters gently lapping its green pastures. St. Bride's
Mound, situated on the riverbank, symbolized the completion of a
physical pilgrimage and the beginning of a spiritual one. Here travelers would be prepared by the maidens of St. Bride to begin an inner

journey that would eventually require them to enter their own under-world at the top of the tor.

The inconsistent preservation of the sacred sites in Glastonbury is typical of many such locations around the world. This, however, seems to be changing as people of both genders recognize the need to restore the sacred balance between the masculine and feminine and hence embrace their own spiritual union within.

Figure 1.8. The mists of Avalon

THE IROQUOIS
CONSTITUTION

Across the ages many ancient traditions have used their understanding of these diverse yet equally important representatives of Triple Goddess to create peaceful, just, and prosperous societies. They selected women as their spiritual leaders, seeing them as representatives of the Mother Goddess possessing far vision, compassionate wisdom, and creative power. The women would then choose men of integrity to be the rulers, mandating them to turn those visions into reality through their practical and physical strength.

Even the Iroquois Constitution, which is the basis for the Constitution of the United States of America, declared that chiefs would be chosen by the women of the tribe.[4] This decision was made because it was seen that only women could selflessly decide what is best for the people as a whole as their vision stretches beyond the immediate future with its superficial profits and toward the sustainable well-being of the next seven generations. It was also understood that only women know the pain of burying the children they have suckled at the breast and only women have the wisdom to decide whether a battle or war is worth the cost of life. Imagine the transformation that would occur around the planet today if women and only women were allowed to vote!

We have seen this compassionate wisdom in action in many war-torn areas around the world where peace has emerged when women come together across the divide. They are driven by an inherent love of the land and its people where there are no divisions, just millions of children all eternally loved by the Great Mother.

Let's now consider each aspect of the Triple Goddess in turn. As we do, let's remember that every goddess embodies the loving power of intuition, which entreats us to follow what is most nurturing to our inner being. As we listen to and follow through on the messages from our own intuition, we are rekindling the eternal fire. We are making choices to move away from situations based on fear that cause us to separate from our soul and toward love so we can express its divine blueprint. All goddesses ask us this one simple question:

Am I acting from love or from fear?

Love connects; fear separates.

2

THE VIRGIN

Contrary to popular belief, the word *virgin* does not reflect a sexually inexperienced girl but instead means "to be complete unto oneself without the need for another to make one whole." Often depicted wearing white, the Virgin radiates a state of energetic perfection wherein she is comfortable with herself and has nothing to hide. An analogy would be that when we buy a jigsaw puzzle, the picture on the front of the box reveals the ultimate expression of wholeness, and yet it is only by working patiently with each piece that the picture is recreated from the building blocks within.

The Virgin can be described as:

- Our spiritual blueprint awaiting manifestation
- Our unrealized or unmanifested self
- Our imagination, containing all the seeds of possibility
- Energetic perfection
- Our holographic self in which everything is essentially present

As we deepen our study of the Virgin within mythology and her relationship to wholeness and purity, it's easy to recognize her within the Christian world as the Virgin Mary. Unfortunately, Mary's radiant pure light of authenticity has often been misinterpreted as possessing man-made ideals of purity, whether of thoughts, words, or deeds, especially when it alludes to sexuality. These twisted dogmas were set in place thousands of years ago by a patriarchy that wanted to control women and determined that, by creating an unattainable role model, women would always feel ashamed of their femininity. They did a good job!

But if we return to the original meaning of the word *virgin,* imagine being in a relationship where you knew you were "complete unto yourself, without the need for another to make you whole." You would still enjoy the creative charge that comes from intimacy but without the fear of rejection, the stickiness of codependency, or the burden of unrealistic expectations that are commonly placed on another person in the mistaken belief that this will make us complete. Imagine the joy of just being in the presence of another soul who embraces his or her implicit wholeness and allows us to do the same.

Such an expression of this pure maiden archetype within our society is relatively uncommon, although it can certainly be witnessed in the crystal or psychic children who embody the principles of the etheric world. These young people are strongly connected to the source of their inspiration and hence to their spiritual blueprint. Thus they appear not to require parenting in the traditional sense. They are self-assured and detached and yet radiate a compassionate presence. We can only imagine how relationships will change as these children enter adulthood. Being "complete unto themselves," their interactions will be free of the heaviness that usually accompanies unspoken expectations and low self-worth.

On an esoteric level, the Virgin's surety of who she is equates to the fact that, dwelling as she does within the unified field where there is no separation, she has no concept of *another* but only an appreciation of *us.*

BRIGID OR BRIGIT OR BRIGHID

Fiery Arrow of Power

It's time to meet Brigid, one of the oldest of the Celtic Virgin goddesses. Her impact on the cycles of creativity and fertility is still remembered at Imbolc, the Celtic festival of the lactating ewes. On February 1 and 2, Imbolc heralds the return of the life-giving forces of spring. Brigid has been known by many names, including Bride, Brigantia, Brigit, Bridey, and Bridget (her Christianized name), which all mean the same thing: "fiery arrow of power." As a much older goddess, she is also known as Brighid, which means "exalted one." There are suggestions of her cultural influence long before the Celtic period. The massive stones used at megalithic sites such as Avebury and Stonehenge are known as bridestones.

Brigid also appears in tales where she shares the year with Cailleach, the Irish and Scottish name for the Divine Hag or Crone. When Cailleach's own son falls in love with Bride and they decide to elope at the winter's end, Cailleach sends fierce storms to prevent their union. Eventually, however, love prevails as the Crone is turned to stone and the couple is free to enjoy their lives together. This story shows the beautiful balance between the Virgin and the Crone, highlighting Cailleach's rule over the winter months and Bride's, or Brigid's, dominion over summer.

In Celtic mythology Brigid is the daughter of the Irish god Dagda, famed for his great power, his cauldron of eternal abundance, and his magical oaken harp, which brings the seasons into order. Many of these skills were passed down to his offspring Brigid, who is often seen as a goddess of fire, her hair shining like the golden rays of the sun.

The ancient people believed that as long as we tend the fire in the heart or hearth and never let it go out, we will always be blessed with good health, abundance, and prosperity. Indeed, it is customary even today for a new bride to be given coals from her mother's fire as a blessing for a fruitful marriage. Many ancient fires were dedicated to Brigid. The most famous of them is still to be found in Kildare, Ireland, where her flame never dies. Yet her fires of continual fertility and creativity are also symbolized in other ways:

- The fires of inspiration, seen especially in poetry and song in which the words carry the frequency of pure insight and intuition.
- The fires of healing found at sacred wells often dedicated to St. Bride or St. Bridget. These waters, rich in minerals, create the perfect balance between fire and water essential for purification of the mind and body and reconnection to the soul. Over time,

many of these wells have become covered over or hidden, but they are now reappearing. Some of the most famous are found at Cullin near Mullingar, at Bride's Mound in Glastonbury, and at St. Bride's Church, London.

Figure 2.1. The enigmatic Bride's Well in Glastonbury, England

Figure 2.2. Brigid's cross, a symbol of new life
and regeneration

- The sexual fire linked to the serpentine kundalini energy, often seen as the inner fire that brings us to the state of self-realization.
- The fire of transformation that mirrors the skills of the blacksmith, who bends and twists metal into a creation of beauty. Brigid, as a master alchemist, uses her fiery power to turn base consciousness into the golden essence of illumination.

The synthesis of Brigid's fiery qualities is, to this day, symbolically woven together in a cross dedicated to her during Imbolc. The specific design of this cross naturally expresses the movement that occurs with the birth of new life as consciousness spirals to the next level.

PALLAS ATHENA
The Keeper of Our Wisdom

Another face of the Virgin is that of Athena, the wisdom keeper of our soul's destiny, guiding us intuitively on our physical journey into wholeness. In Greek mythology she was known as the goddess Athena, although her roots stretch back into earlier times when she was known as Pallas Athena. She emerged originally from the element of water—the Great Mother—similar to many of the other great maiden goddesses. It is even thought that she lived among us as an enlightened being or ascended master during the Lemurian civilization, over one hundred thousand years ago.

Athena represents the principles of truth and wisdom that, contrary to the opinions of pragmatists and fundamentalists, are not set in stone but instead emerge out of our own unique creative experiences within the holographic universe. Athena speaks to us through our intuition. This still, small voice of inner reason or knowing maintains the connection to our spiritual blueprint, urging us to fulfill our destiny in the world.

She also helps us have the courage to manifest a dream into reality, to extract gems of wisdom from past experiences, and to allow old habits to die so healthy shoots of new life can appear.

With the advent of the Greek civilization and its strong physical and intellectual bias, it was determined that if Pallas Athena was to continue to guide her people, her persona must be altered so as not to threaten patriarchal beliefs. Thus her story changed. She was no longer born from the feminine waters but from the head of her father, Zeus. She was fully armored, protecting her femininity, and prepared to channel her wisdom through the mind.

Over time, and despite the masculine tendency to solidify wisdom into dogma, the goddess managed to keep her timeless qualities of truth and wisdom alive through the arts, body-centered wisdom, and intuition. Yet her hold was tenuous and such inner knowing was often viewed as "feminine fancy," implying that because it does not come from "reasoned thinking" it must be delusional, emotional, or a little crazy. Fortunately, Jung and other great psychologists arrived on the scene just in time to bear witness to the archetypal energy of Pallas Athena. Through their research they showed that it's impossible to understand the psyche if we only view it through the lens of the logical mind.

Pallas Athena is slowly returning to her rightful place within our

Figure 2.3. Pallas Athena,
a seminal deity down through time

consciousness, although interestingly it is women who often have more difficulty letting down their masculine mental defenses and trusting Pallas Athena's inner wisdom.

3

THE MOTHER

Of the three faces of the Triple Goddess it would probably be true to say that it's the Mother who is best known and accepted within most cultures. She is seen as the loving and generous nurturer of our needs, feeding us from her abundant fruitfulness. She is known as Demeter or Artemis to the Greeks, Lakshmi to the Hindus, Tara to both the Indians and Tibetans, Kwan Yin to Buddhists, Nu Kua to the Chinese, Cybele to the ancient Turks, Diana to the Romans, Freya to the people of northern Europe, Astarte to the ancient people of the Middle East, Isis and Hathor to the Egyptians, Inanna to the Sumerians, and Mary to the Christians, to cite just a few of the names she's been given.

ARTEMIS
The Fecund Goddess

She is commonly represented as a large-breasted woman, epitomized by the Greek goddess Artemis, whose entire torso is covered with breasts.

During the sixth century BCE a magnificent temple was built in honor of Artemis at Ephesus (in present-day Turkey). It was considered one of the seven wonders of the ancient world. Today, all that's left of her beautiful temple are a few pillars and the original foundation stones.

Figure 3.1. The fecund goddess Artemis

DIANA

Grandmother of God

As Christianity spread across Europe and other areas bordering the Mediterranean, such sacred places of worship were either destroyed or transformed into churches dedicated to Mother Mary. To the Romans, Artemis became known as Diana or Di-Anna, which meant "grandmother of God." With the arrival of Christianity, Di-Anna was demoted to Anna, "the grandmother of Jesus." Yet the worship of the goddess Artemis/Diana lives on in the Festival of Candles, which takes place annually throughout Europe on August 15 and symbolizes her promise of eternal life for those who follow her loving example. It is interesting to note this same date is now associated with the Christian

Church's celebration of the Assumption of Mary, in which the message is essentially the same.

HATHOR

The Heavenly Cow

In other cultures we find the Mother represented by a multi-nippled, horned animal such as a cow or goat. This representation gives rise to a popular emblem of the mother aspect called the *horn of plenty* or *cornucopia,* from which pours the fruits of the Earth.

In Hinduism, the mother aspect of Kali is symbolized as a white-horned, milk-giving moon cow. In Egypt, Hathor, the mother of all gods and goddesses, is commonly depicted wearing cow's horns and offering her breasts with both hands. The high esteem in which Hathor was held in the Egyptian culture comes from her representation as the heavenly cow whose udder produces the whiteness of the Milky Way and who daily gives birth to the sun god Horus-Ra, her golden calf.

Figure 3.2. Hathor, the heavenly cow
From E. A. Budge's *The Nile: Notes for Travellers in Egypt* (London: Harrison and Sons, 1902), pg. 189; under Wikimedia Commons license CC BY-SA 2.5

HATHOR.

Thus it is no surprise to learn that, as the Israelites left the land where the goddess Hathor was honored as the source of continual sustenance, they took the opportunity—while Moses was away receiving the Ten Commandments—to melt down their gold and build a golden calf, hoping that Hathor would continue to bless their journey.

This same theme of the Mother being depicted as a milk-giver gave rise to the name Italy, meaning "calf land," suggesting that it had been birthed by the Goddess. Even earlier myths from Japan, the Middle East, and India speak of the universe as being curdled into shape from cows' milk, leading to the Hindu creative myth Samudra Manthan (the churning of the sea of milk), which we will discuss later.

DEMETER

Goddess of Agriculture and Harvest

One final example of mother energy is the Greek goddess Demeter (the Roman goddess Ceres), who was goddess of agriculture and of the harvest, sister of Zeus, and mother of Kore/Persephone. Her name comes from the Greek letter *delta,* which means a "triangle," and *meter,* which means "mother." Together they represent the vulva of the Great Mother, reminding us of the esteemed position she held among the deities as Mother of the Greek culture. As daughter of Cronus and Rhea (also a Mother Goddess), Demeter taught humanity how to live in right relationship with Mother Earth by valuing her ability to transform seeds into abundant harvests and then allowing the land to rest so it might renew itself during the winter months.

Apart from the cornucopia, Demeter is also often seen with a multi-seeded head of wheat and a golden, double-headed ax. Her symbolic animals include the pig, dragon, serpent, and turtledove, all of which are linked to other powerful Mother Goddess figures.

Despite a somewhat childlike belief that the Mother is a benign being whose bountiful gifts are constantly available to us, whatever we do it's important to understand that she holds the power over when

Figure 3.3. Demeter, goddess of agriculture and the harvest
From fourth edition of *Meyers Konversationslexikon* (1885–90)

and where to create. The great Zeus found this out at his expense when he gave permission to his brother Hades to abduct Demeter's daughter Kore/Persephone and take her into the underworld. Demeter showed her displeasure by causing the entire land to become barren.

It is the mother energy that provides the energy behind every manifested form we see in the world, whether it causes a blade of grass to quiver or hot lava to flow from a mighty volcano. In human terms, this mother energy can be seen as our emotions—energy in motion—that nurture and stimulate our thoughts and dreams to take form. Without this force even the most focused attention and greatest determination will amount to nothing.

Honoring the mother aspect of the Triple Goddess is not just a case of "a quick word of thanks." We have to learn to take nothing for granted and respect her essential elements of earth, water, air, fire, and ether. Welcoming the sun in the morning and the stars and moon at night as if it's the first time you've been in their presence honors this mother energy. Celebrating every phase of Creation—whether it's the growth period, the moments of full bloom, the harvest, or the dying energy—is the best way to ensure sustainable growth and abundance whether for your family, a business, a relationship, your garden, or all who share this beautiful Mother Earth.

4

THE CRONE

Having honored the Mother, we will now move on to the Crone. Given that she is both revered and feared within most cultures, there is no doubt that of all the aspects of the Triple Goddess, the Crone is probably the most difficult for an individual to accept and integrate. Known variously as the Old Woman, the Wise One, the Dark Mother, and the Hag, she is commonly portrayed as being bloodthirsty, sexually promiscuous, and extremely ugly. The territory she rules is seen as chaotic, representing the unknown and untamed aspects of our nature, which is why those who like to stay in control find her appearance in their lives so disturbing.

Representations of this powerful feminine archetype include Kali the destroyer, Cerridwen the corpse-eating sow, Sekhmet the fire-breathing lion, Isis the vulture queen, Morgan Le Fay the death queen, and Persephone the destroyer. No wonder she has acquired such a reputation! All represent death, winter, destruction, and doom. Indeed, the Grim Reaper, seen brandishing his scythe as a sign of impending death, originates from an ancient Scythian goddess whose symbol, like that of many of the death goddesses, is the dying crescent moon.

As we will discover, each cultural myth surrounding the Crone offers a different perspective of her archetypal energy, although all agree that this is one powerful lady!

SEKHMET

The Lion Goddess

It is believed that the Sphinx, which stands on the Giza Plateau, was originally built in the image of this powerful lion goddess, eleven thousand years ago, to protect the pharaohs of Upper Egypt. It is said that Sekhmet's breath created the hot desert winds, and that arrows of fire darted from her eyes.

Let's look at an interesting myth that describes her relationship with the god Ra, a much younger deity who emerged around 3000 BCE. This

Figure 4.1. Sekhmet, awe-inspiring Crone

Photo of statue of Sekhmet in British Museum from Flickr,
by virtusincertus under license CC BY 2.0

time was notable in that it marked the start of the suppression and sub-jugation of the feminine. As a result, predynastic goddesses were often immersed in the new patriarchal culture as a wife or a slave or otherwise eclipsed completely. In this story, Ra appears to have created Sekhmet and rules over her, despite the fact she is the older deity. He demands that she use her destructive elements to do his bidding.

Ra, the sun god, creates Sekhmet from his fiery eye and calls on her to destroy the mortals who conspire against him. When he sees blood running in the streets, he knows he must stop her before she goes too far, and hence he produces a red ochre beer. In her thirst for blood, she drinks it, and becomes intoxicated, immediately falling asleep and reverting into a benign and loving goddess.

Clearly the patriarchy was very unhappy with the crone aspect of the Great Mother and especially the dark destructive and transforma-tive power of women particularly evident during menstruation and the dark moon days around the new moon. Ra tried to use this power to his own advantage but instead became fearful of the chaos and destruction he had unleashed and eventually had to silence her. This is a wonderful warning for us all: if you choose to call on the Crone or Dark Goddess, be ready for the chaos she may bring to your life in the name of love! She is only too willing to burn away any external beliefs or identities that stubbornly define and limit us, so we can happily merge into the love of the Great Mother and her ocean of possibilities.

Ra, like many leaders, wanted to control the Crone and even make fun of her chaotic nature, so he could show his followers who was boss. But the Crone is nobody's servant and cannot be silenced. Today, she is sending a warning to the patriarchy that she is reconnecting humans to their own source of creative power, and when this happens there will be no need for a pharaoh or leader to tell us what we can or cannot do!

Similar to other myths that describe the killing of serpents or dragons—symbols of crone power—Ra's attempts to nullify Sekhmet's power are feeble in the presence of this great crone!

HEL AND PELE

Goddesses of Regeneration

Named after the great goddess Hel, hell is one of the most feared places in religious mythology. However, unlike the Christians, the ancient Norse people saw the underworld not as a place of retribution and punishment but as a womb of regeneration. The earliest shrines to Hel were, in fact, uterine-shaped caverns often connected to underground hot water streams fed by a nearby volcano. Other caves were connected to a glacier, suggesting that Hel is comfortable in all extremes of temperature. To the Norse, everybody—including gods and goddesses— had to pass through the domain of this goddess, and therefore it was never a place to be feared.

In the Pacific region, Mother Death is still believed to live within a fire mountain. Hence we meet the Dark Goddess Pele who, like Hel, keeps the souls of the dead alive in a regenerative fire until they are ready to be reborn. Instead of terrorizing with the threat of eternal torture—like the Christian notion of hell—in mythical terms Pele's cauldron or volcanic caldera promises eternal life. With this in mind, the next time someone tells you to "Go to hell," remember that they are in fact giving you a wonderful blessing. Thus you may reply: "Thank you, I will! May *you* be so lucky!"

One other interesting fact associated with the goddess Hel is that, in many traditions, we learn of the lords of death who, wearing a *hel-met* or mask of invisibility, are able to pass through the underworld undetected by the Dark Goddess, thereby escaping her wrath. Having achieved this feat, they are often called the *gems within the womb*—similar to the *Buddhist jewel within the lotus* that symbolizes the brilliant light of the Divine that radiates from a soul living in his or her Ka body. We now know it is the pineal gland that has the potential to produce such light, creating a brilliant cloak of invisibility and immortality.

ARTEMIS

The Huntress

Artemis is a Triple Goddess appearing as the Virgin, as a free and independent spirit running through the woods at night with her hunting dogs, needing only her intuition to guide her. As the Crone, she embodies the power of life over death, seen as the huntress ready to kill the very creatures she has brought into existence. Yet her power is not malevolent but comes from a place of fate that has no connection to emotions, desires, or whims.

To Artemis, there is a time for everything: If it is time to die, we die. It is because of this clear, unattached focus that she is assigned to be the patron of midwifery, birth being seen as a point of transition when life hangs in the balance, and only the Crone can decide the baby's destiny.

One of the best-known tales of this Greek goddess highlights this philosophical approach to life, although the tale has been corrupted by those who prefer to see Artemis with human emotions rather than wearing the detached face of fatalism.

A young hunter comes upon the goddess bathing naked. Apparently offended by his effrontery and humiliated by her vulnerability, Artemis immediately turns him into a stag and encourages his own dogs to tear him apart until he is killed.

Sadly the interpretations of such myths are often biased toward a belief that men and women distrust each other and may end up destroying each other. In truth, Artemis is not bothered by whether the young man sees her naked or not—she is a Crone! She is the marker of time, and by killing the hunter, she is re-enacting an ancient Minoan sacred ritual where annually as winter approaches the "stag king god"— representing the dying sun—must die, allowing for the birth of the new sun at the winter solstice. There are many traditional tales that tell a similar story, including the death and resurrection of Jesus, or Yeshua. This demonstrates that for continual peace and prosperity there needs to be a harmonic cyclical relationship between feminine and masculine energies.

Artemis's association with fate is reinforced by the fact that she is identified with the Great She-Bear, the constellation Ursa Major, which contains the well-known Big Dipper or Plough. Her apparent movement through the sky highlights her position as the protector of the axis mundi, or the pole of the world, demarcated in the heavens by the North Star or polestar. For ancient peoples, the beginning of each new season was marked by the position of the tail of the Great She-Bear, Artemis, acting as the eternal clock.

The Dark Goddess is calling "time" for all of us now. She is not interested in our bargaining tactics, excuses, or entreaties, especially those linked to our small ego's desire not to upset the status quo. It is time to move on . . . whether we are ready to or not.

MAUT or MUT
The Vulture Goddess

For several years during meditation I had the distinct impression of having a beak, a crown or tuft of hair, and beautiful, sleek feathers. I had even "felt" myself riding the thermals high up in the clear sky, my wings outstretched, looking down on the tiny moving dots on the ground. A few years ago the impressions were so strong that I decided to ask for help from a friend, a wise and wonderful Hawaiian kahuna.

He drove me to the lava tubes created by Pele's powerful volcanic eruptions on the Big Island of Hawaii and suggested I take the winding path down to the bottom of the caldera and allow the natural environment to work its magic on me. As I descended, I opened myself to the consciousness of the bird and felt my body transform immediately until I possessed a powerful beak, keen, piercing eyes, and sharp talons. Believing that I'd shapeshifted into an eagle and rather proud of the fact, I asked within: "Who are you?"

The reply took me by surprise: "I am a vulture."

"Oh no," I said, deflated, as all my prejudices rose to the surface. "How can I tell this holy man waiting for me at the top of the path that I am a vulture?" Fortunately, within seconds of that judgmental thought, my curiosity moved me to ask, "You hover in the sky, waiting for animals to die?"

As soon as this thought left my mind, I felt my vulture wings shake, demanding respect. "Yes, you're right. I eat the dead, but not the living. I clean the bones of every animal, freeing each from its earthly attachments so its spirit can return to the source and be reborn. Only those who fear death or have forgotten the regenerative cycles see us as ugly pests. Others welcome us with open arms."

I was humbled by its comments, aware that I hadn't always looked favorably upon this beautiful creature.

"Our eyesight is keen," the vulture continued, "which enables us to see over a much greater distance than almost any other bird. This allows us to not only see objects on the ground but also to observe the beauty and perfect harmony of our multidimensional existence; it is so close you could touch it and yet, for a limited human mind it might as well be in another universe."

Humbled by the wisdom of this mighty bird, my new teacher, I returned to where my friend was waiting and proceeded to tell him what had occurred. "Of course," he said as I finished. "The vulture is the condor, a bird of spirit who lives and moves between the dimensions much as Hermes moved between the worlds delivering the messages of the gods. The vulture can live in both worlds, those of the living and the dead, and is especially adapted to clearing the way so others can follow, even if that means cleaning the meat off the bones of the dead."

Since then I have learned that the vulture is in fact one of the oldest totem animals of the Crone and is known in Egypt as the angel of death. Several cultures, including that of the Tibetans and the ancient Iranians, would not bury their dead but preferred to lay them in an open-topped "tower of silence" so the vultures could perform the last rites. Part of the reason for this was that the hard earth and desert were unsuitable for an earth-based burial. However, the Iranians also built these towers to honor the moon goddess Mah, believing that the vultures would carry the dead to the heavenly realms. Even when physical burial was introduced by the Persians, the body was still broken apart by the vultures before it was interred.

To the Egyptians the vulture-headed goddess was seen as the origin of all things. She was embodied in figures such as Mut and Isis, the latter often appearing as a vulture holding the ankh, the cross of life, in one of her talons. It is as the vulture that she tears apart the flesh of her dead consort, Osiris, and then reincarnates him in her womb (reassembles the pieces) before giving birth to him as Horus, the son and heir. Thus we see that Isis's womb is also a tomb, providing both the power to nurture and give birth and the power to destroy. Indeed the name *sarcophagus*, where the Egyptians often laid their dead, means "flesh-eating coffin."

THE VALKYRIES

Crows, Hawks, Mares, and Swans

We meet other corpse-eating goddesses in the tales of the Valkyries, who, as attendants of the Norse god Odin, take the form of carrion-eating birds such as crows and ravens. Indeed, the word *crone* is thought to derive from *coronis*, meaning "a crow." Alchemically, the appearance of these birds in our life represents the first signs that the Dark Goddess is calling.

The Valkyries could also shapeshift into hawks, swans, and even mares. Indeed, the word *nightmare* comes from the belief that such a frightening dream occurs after a visitation to the underworld, riding on the back of the Dark Goddess. All three animals mentioned above are associated with an ease of movement between the worlds. Thus the shamans of old wore swan feathers to assist their journey between the dimensions. Therefore it is not surprising to learn that the figure of an old woman riding on the back of a swan is seen in the contours of the landscape of the Isle of Avalon—Glastonbury—which is known to be a portal into the underworld.[1]

There are many stories pertaining to the swan, with the most famous perhaps being that of the ballet *Swan Lake*. Written by Tchaikovsky, it tells of the powerful attraction between the heir to the throne, Prince Siegfried, and Princess Odette. She has been turned into a swan by day and a woman by night by the evil sorcerer Von Rothbart. Even though this is a relatively modern tale and has various endings that are both romantic and tragic, it signifies the spell that the Dark Goddess, the swan, holds over the young king, who knows he is ultimately destined to succumb to her clutches. It is interesting to note that in this particular version of the story, the princess's alternating persona is contrary to the archetypal interpretation of the myth, which is that we are human by day and swans by night, free to fly within our dreams.

In other traditional tales, we hear how the wings of the swan are seized and hidden, trapping the creature in this physical world. Some scholars relate this story to the entrapment of a woman during her childbearing years, unable to fly until her wings are returned at menopause.

Finally, there are myths that tell of the wicked witch, the Crone, who turns men into swans, signifying their descent into the underworld. Eventually, they are returned to human form by a maiden, but only after the maiden herself has gone through various trials to achieve their release. As you will read later, this story is symbolic of the Sumerian goddess Inanna's descent into the underworld and reminds us that it is only through the continual interplay between our Crone and Virgin—where one gives way to the other—that our masculine aspect will eventually be reborn into eternal life.

All of these stories touch on the true esoteric meaning of attaining our "wings," which describes the drawing up of energy into the third eye chakra, or *ajna*. The two lobes of this chakra (mirroring the two lobes of the pituitary gland) fill with energy until the "wings" are powerful enough to transport our essence to the pineal gland, ultimately leading to the eternal realms. We will look at this in more detail in a later chapter.

KALI

The Destroyer

Even though Kali is the Hindu Triple Goddess, she is best known for her dark embodiment. She sits astride the body of her dead consort, Shiva, and eats his entrails while her yoni, or vulva, devours his lingam, or penis. More than any other goddess, Kali symbolizes the archetypal image of the birth-death Mother whose womb is also a tomb, giving life and death to her children. This poignantly reminds us that at the

Figure 4.2. Kali with the head of one of her victims

A tantric form of the Hindu goddess Kali, folio from *A Book of Iconography* (Nepal, seventeenth century), released by the Los Angeles County Museum of Art

same moment a woman gives birth she is also consigning her child to the inevitability of death.

To Western eyes Kali is often seen as the she-demon, yet any projection upon her is simply a reflection of what we fear most within ourselves. Even the powerful Vishnu saw himself as just a mere construct of her maternal substance, with her timeless ocean of blood being the source of all Creation.

MARY MAGDALENE
A Vessel for the Transformation of Jesus

Throughout Europe it is not uncommon to find cathedrals dedicated to the Black Madonna, the most famous being those in Chartres, France; Czestochowa, Poland; and Montserrat, Spain. There is some question as to who the Black Madonna actually represents, for statues of her often depict her pregnant or with a child on her lap. The people of France strongly believe this is Mary Magdalene, the wife of Jesus and mother of his child.

Yet if this is the Magdalene, she must be acknowledged as far more than just the wife to Jesus. She was a highly evolved soul, a high priestess, trained in the temples of Isis in the ways of the Crone. Here death and resurrection were fully recognized as being the pathway to enlightenment and the elixir of life.[2]

Through her "marriage" to Jesus, she offered him her womb/tomb—her cauldron—for his journey into the underworld, where he met his own demons and tempters. Here he allowed her powers of transformation to work upon his psyche, tearing down any barriers that prevented him from knowing himself in his perfect state. Each time he came face-to-face with his own demons, he found within his heart a place of unconditional love that increasingly strengthened his core. Through recurrent journeys into the underworld, his Ka or light body became stronger until he was able to undergo physical death and, within three days, resurrect fully within his light body—the expression of immortality.

The ability to contain Jesus's energy as he went through this process highlights Mary Magdalene's own level of enlightenment and the fact that she must have journeyed into the underworld to meet and integrate her own demons before becoming the vessel for his transformation.

So is she in fact the Black Madonna? Having delved into her history in recent years, I'm almost certain she was a woman of high standing—possibly a princess—from the land of Ethiopia and the lineage of the Queen of Sheba, a powerful matrilineal race. If this is true, she was indeed black, foreign, educated, powerful, and rich, a combination that would not have gone down well with the patriarchal populace of that time!

OTHER SYMBOLS ASSOCIATED WITH THE CRONE

The Cauldron

Many goddesses possess a magical cauldron or pot of blood, representing the womb of the cosmic Mother. Apart from the goddesses already mentioned, the cauldron is also associated with the Welsh goddess Branwen, the Celtic Cerridwen, the Irish Morgan Le Fay, and the Babylonian fate goddess Sitis, mother of the stars.

As portrayed in Shakespeare's *Macbeth,* the cauldron is usually in the care of three witches or three *wyrd* (wise) sisters, symbolizing the Triple Goddess. At other times, three cauldrons are depicted. Whether one or three, the cauldron's purpose is clear: it is the container of the wise blood, the mead of regeneration, or the ambrosia of eternal life—in other words, it is the place where death and birth repeatedly occur, ultimately leading to immortality. Where is this cauldron to be found within a human body? It is the womb or uterus that miraculously can transform a few cells into a beautiful baby and also transform emotions into menstrual blood to be released during a woman's moon-time or period. This is crone power at its finest.

The Apple

One final symbol connected to the Crone is the apple, with strong links to the festival of Halloween and the Celtic Samhain, when the Crone, as Cailleach, takes over rule of the Earth from the Virgin at the start of winter. Many other ancient traditions also consider the apple as a symbol of death and rebirth through the mystery of darkness. To the Celtic people, their sacred site of transformation was Avalon or Glastonbury, the "Isle of Apples." To the ancient Scandinavians, apples ensured resurrection, so they would insert an apple into the mouth of a sacrificed boar during the winter solstice to ease the birth of the new sun. For the Greeks, the great goddess Hera owned a garden of golden apples that bestowed the gift of immortality to all who managed to pass by her fierce dragon Ladon and eat the fruit.

One of the reasons the apple has been treated with such reverence is that when cut transversely, the core with its seeds forms a perfect pentagram, a magical symbol of resurrection, lifting us above a physical world consisting of four elements and into the world of spiritual magic, the world of ether.

Yet the Crone offers us this warning: to reach this place, we must be willing to dissolve the flesh from our old stories in her cauldron of fire and then be nurtured by the flesh of our own creations or experiences. Are you ready to eat the golden fruit?

5

THE BIRTH OF
THE ONE MIND

Merging with the Masculine

Ancient Creation myths speak of the Triple Goddess as the One Thing out of which emerges her consort or masculine counterpart, known to alchemists as the One Mind. This represents the *focus to create,* also seen as attention, direction, or the conscious mind, without which the feminine *force or power to create* stays in its amorphous form.

THE LAW OF ATTRACTION

Together, the feminine *force* to create and the masculine *focus* to create give rise to *intention:*

FORCE + FOCUS = INTENTION

A useful analogy may be found in the cooking of a meal. The ingredients, the heated oven, and the recipe contain the dynamic energetic blueprint of the finished product and embody the feminine *force* or energy. It is the masculine *focus* that brings the motivation or willpower to actively fertilize the plan, eventually bringing the meal to the table. Working together, the masculine and the feminine create our concept of reality.

When force plus focus lead to the outcome we had already envisioned we call it synchronicity and recognize it as part of our journey toward oneness, especially when the outcome is positive. Yet when the same process of combining force and focus results in a perceived negative result it is not uncommon to defiantly deny any connection between ourselves as the creator and the unfortunate manifestation, preferring to see the outcome as mere coincidence.

Within the realms of creativity, we cannot pick and choose what we decide to own. Everything that causes us to have an emotional reaction reflects a part of our own spiritual blueprint. This is based on the understanding that our purpose on Earth is to manifest fully the unique aspect of the Great Mother that we carry in order for her to know herself through us—in other words, to express heaven on earth. Hence, as we move through the world we project our energetic blueprint or aura into the environment. Naturally this attracts people and situations into our lives that ensure the blueprint is brought into manifestation. This is the true meaning of the law of attraction, which is not derived from a mentally or emotionally based desire but from the undeniable intention of the soul, causing us to receive what we need, not what we want!

When our emotions and senses are activated by something pleasant, we recognize the part of the self that is mirrored in the situation and we experience positive resonance. However, when we meet a projection of ourselves that's unpleasant, we are less willing to be accountable for or accepting of our creations, often feeling angry, defensive, judgmental, or fearful toward the offending situation or person. Yet whatever we judge in others is what we fear finding in ourselves.

Like it or not, whatever aspect of the self that belongs to us will not go away. It is instead awaiting integration, and at this specific time, twenty-six thousand years of our creations are lining up to be remembered. Indeed, the road to immortality asks that we meet and embrace all aspects of ourselves until we can stand fully radiant in our light body.

In summary, there are two primary archetypal energies out of which all Creation is born and from which our dreams will ultimately reach manifestation. Here are their different names:

One Thing + One Mind

Divine Mother/Goddess + Divine Father/God

Soul + Spirit

Chaos + Structure

Emotion + Logic

Force to Create + Focus to Create

Power + Purpose

In the world of duality both aspects have equal importance and each impacts everything we do. The masculine face provides our world with structure and stability mainly through identity, thoughts, laws, and beliefs. The feminine face provides movement and opportunity largely through creativity, inspiration, and intuition. Problems arise when one aspect is given preference over the other, causing the one that is suppressed to rise up in order to reestablish its rightful position.

When the world becomes too structured and lacks spontaneity and growth, the feminine face offers turmoil, which shakes things up and offers new perspectives from the realms of imagination. In a similar way, when mayhem or confusion is rampant, events occur that force us to make decisions or set priorities, thereby bringing masculine order out of the chaos. A continual flow of energy between the masculine and feminine principles is the force that creates healthy, reciprocally rewarding relationships where all aspects are respected and honored.

THE EGO IS BORN

As the Creation myth continues, we learn that the One Mind and the One Thing express their love by breathing life into each other, thereby creating a vesica piscis out of which the ego, the creative light of manifestation, is born.

Without an ego there can be no spiritual journey, for:

It is through the growth and development of the ego that energy is transformed into matter, creating what we perceive as reality; the phase of inspiration. It is through the ego's willingness to

*die that the essence of the experience is gifted back to the source,
reminding us that nothing really matters: the phase of expiration.*

This cycle between spirit and matter or heaven and earth is also
known as the *hero myth* in which the ego passes through several stages of
evolution (inspiration) and dissolution (expiration), taking on different
roles as it dives in and out of the Great Mother's ocean of possibilities.
The intimate balance between the masculine (focus to create) and the
feminine (force to create) is reflected in the interplay of energies between
the various signs of the zodiac.

The word *zodiac* is derived from a Greek word meaning "circle of
little animals." Although not all the symbols of the zodiac are animals,
the Indo-European cultures developed a zodiac of twelve signs or constellations of stars through which the sun appears to pass during its
yearly journey across the heavens on what is known as *the ecliptic*.

With the twelve constellations each thirty degrees apart, each symbolizes a particular phase of the mythological story of the sun-hero and
subconsciously impacts this planet and its people. Starting with Pisces,
the fish, the constellations alternate between feminine-negative and
masculine-positive—there are six of each polarity in the zodiac.

- **Virgin:** containing the seed of potential, our creative blueprint (**Pisces**)
- **Puer:** the innocent boy-child, inexperienced but eager to learn (**Aries**)
- **Mother:** offering nurturing and support for the journey (**Taurus**)
- **Hero:** grasping the dual nature of consciousness, physical and spiritual (**Gemini**)
- **Crone:** meeting and embracing the mirrors of our existence (**Cancer**)
- **King:** the crowning and full expression of our blueprint (**Leo**)
- **Virgin/Triple Goddess:** guiding us toward introspection and contemplation (**Virgo**)
- **Lover:** offering compassion, fairness, reason, and self-discipline (**Libra**)*

---

*The sign of Libra represents balance and is the synthesis of the fierce love of the Mother
face of the Triple Goddess with the courage and determination of the hero-king. Hence
the designation as simply the "lover" that exists in all of us.

- **Crone/Triple Goddess:** embracing inner riches (**Scorpio**)
- **Sage:** instilling wisdom, truth, and insight based on detachment from form (**Sagittarius**)
- **Triple Goddess:** transforming matter into pure essence (**Capricorn**)
- **Magician:** living in both worlds as wand holder, shapeshifter, and shaman (**Aquarius**)
- **Great Mother:** presenting nothingness, the end and the beginning (**Pisces**)

These wonderful characters will be our guides as we journey along the path to immortality in part 3 of this book.

SACRED NUMBERS OF CREATIVITY

The emergence of everything out of the Great Mother is expressed in a sequence called *Fibonacci numbers,* believed to underpin the success of any creative enterprise. Each number except the first is produced from the addition of the two previous numbers:

$$1 \quad 1 \quad 2 \quad 3 \quad 5 \quad 8 \quad 13 \quad 21 \quad 34 \quad 55 \quad 89 \ldots$$

The relationship between the numbers is eventually seen to result in the *golden mean,* in which a number is 0.618 times greater than the previous number, stretching into infinity. This is also known as the *golden ratio.* Such a fundamental mathematical equation for creative evolution is expressed in natural phenomena such as the pattern of seeds in the head of a sunflower.

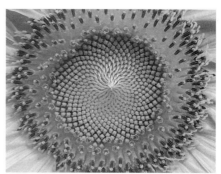

Figure 5.1. A sunflower, nature's manifestation of the golden spiral

These seeds are arranged in logarithmic spirals flowing out from the center in both directions. If the seeds along the clockwise and counterclockwise spirals are counted, it is found that the totals represent two successive numbers in the Fibonacci series, such as 34 and 55 seeds. This golden spiral is seen in other natural forms such as the scaly plates of a pineapple, the nautilus shell, the seeds of a pinecone, and the spiral of the Milky Way, to mention just a few. It is believed that nature appreciates the golden spiral as being not only pleasing to the eye but offering quantity without sacrificing quality.

When we review our present understanding of the Creation myth, we see that it also follows this ancient mathematical system:

- In the Beginning is the Great Mother: **1**
- She gives birth to herself, the One Thing: **1**
- The One Thing gives birth to the One Mind: **2**
- Together, they create the ego: **3**
- Out of the ego come the five stages of manifestation (Aries to Leo): **5**
- These are followed by the stages of growth into transformation (Aries to Scorpio): **8**
- Together, these stages represent the complete cycle of creativity from birth into rebirth (Pisces to Pisces): **13**

These last three numbers (5, 8, 13) represent the different levels of initiation through which we must pass if we are to achieve the ultimate goal of immortality. They strongly relate to the awakening of not just the seven well-known chakras but also ultimately the twelve chakras, some of which radiate beyond the physical form. Thus the number 5—the pentagram—represents change that occurs when we master and synthesize the four elements, lifting spirit from the confines of a purely material existence into the element of ether. (Astrologically this is Aries to Leo.)

The number 8, the octagon, represents the number of notes in an octave and symbolizes the sacred marriage between spirit and matter,

Figure 5.2. The pentagram, or five-pointed star

heaven and earth, or in-breath (inspiration) and out-breath (expiration), leading to the extraction of light wisdom. (Astrologically this is Aries to Scorpio.)

The number 13, the number of transformation, represents completion and the serpent that eats its own tail—the Ouroboros. Once we understand the esoteric nature of these cycles, it is not difficult to imagine why 13 is often depicted as unlucky by those who desire to wield power over others. For, if we have the courage to become the hero-king and then allow ourselves to die into no-thingness so we can once again tap into the source of Creation—the Great Mother—there will be no need for gurus, priests, or leaders to act as intermediaries between ourselves and our divine self. When we acknowledge 13 as being auspicious, we remember that first and foremost we are immortal, without the need of an outside authority to make us whole. (Astrologically this is Pisces to Pisces.)

As our hero's journey unfolds, we will see that our own creative process follows the exact proportions of sacred geometry and that, despite our frequently limited and subjective perspective of life, everything is perfect.

Let's now examine a Hindu myth that beautifully illustrates the journey we must all take to achieve the oneness of immortality.

SAMUDRA MANTHAN

The Churning of the Sea of Milk

This wonderful Hindu hero myth is one of the most famous episodes in the Puranas and is celebrated every twelve years in a festival called Kumbha Mela.

Constant warring occurs between two groups, the Devas and the Asuras. One group has divine qualities and the other consists of demons. Tired of battling, the Devas call on Vishnu for a solution and are advised to churn the sea of milk and hence produce the nectar of immortality, providing them with the obvious upper hand. There is one snag to the solution, however: they cannot do this without the help of the Asuras, so the two groups strike a temporary truce.

Each agrees to hold one end of the snake Vasuki, which is wrapped around the mountain Mandara, and to alternately pull on it, causing the milk to churn. The plan proceeds well until all of a sudden the mountain begins to sink into the sea and the Devas once again cry out to Vishnu for help. He sends himself as Kurma the turtle to support the mountain from beneath, and the process continues.

The first substance to emerge is a highly venomous poison, a by-product of the pain the serpent experiences when pulled in both directions. The only being who can safely swallow the venom is the god Shiva, who clears the way for other things to emerge from the milk. The Devas and Asuras watch as a variety of gift-bearing gods and goddesses step out of the sea. The final god is the divine doctor who carries the nectar of immortality, or amrita.

As the Asuras surge forward to partake of the elixir, the Devas call upon Vishnu to distract their enemy while they drink. He agrees and transforms himself into the glamorous and alluring Mohini, drawing the attention of the Asuras away from the cup. Yet Rahu, an Asura, is not fooled by the ploy and, seizing the cup, he swallows some of the drink. In an instant, Mohini turns and immediately cuts off his head, causing only the top half of Rahu to become immortal while the rest remains untamed and uncouth.

Hence, the Devas achieve their immortality and we receive important insights from a Hindu perspective about the steps we need to take to reach a state of immortality through right relationship with the Mother and her ocean of possibilities or, in this case, her sea of milk.

The Symbolism of Samudra Manthan

The story clearly illustrates the multifaceted, dual nature of our existence, which must be honored and respected if we are ever to know oneness.

- The sea of milk or ocean of possibilities is the Great Mother, the One Thing, the collective consciousness, the plenum of potentiality, and a reflection of our multidimensional existence.
- Vishnu represents the One Mind and is seen as the preserver or the all-pervading one who directs and sustains activities within the universe.
- The Devas and Asuras epitomize the duality of life emerging from the union between the One Thing and the One Mind. These two poles of existence, characterized by the positive and negative aspects of our personality, must work together in a harmonic and integrated fashion in order for us to attain self-realization.
- Vasuki, the serpent, symbolizes the *force* or *power* inherent in every facet of the One Thing activated by the focusing ability of the One Mind. The story emphasizes that power on its own is neutral and can be used equally by both the dark and the light. Indeed, it is only when we harness the power of both sides working together that we are able to produce the elixir of immortality. Hear me when I say that "both light and dark are required to work in harmony to bring forth the riches of the eternal world."
- Mandara, the mountain, symbolizes focused presence, concentration, or attentiveness. The word *mandara* is made up of two words, *mana* (mind) and *dara* (a single line), which together mean "holding the mind in one line."

- Kurma the turtle is called upon to support the mountain (focused attention) when it starts to sink, thus representing inner work or focus. This reminds us that without the strengthening qualities of introspection and contemplation pure concentration is unstable and cannot be maintained, causing the focus of our attention to fall back into the sea of pure illusion.

- The poison reminds us that as we turn within and face our own demons for the first time, it is not uncommon for deep inner turmoil and painful disharmony to emerge. Psychologically these demons represent suppressed, archetypal complexes that are held within our psyche from other lives or from ancestral karma and have become separated from us through fear and shame. As part of the remembering, these aspects of ourselves must be met, accepted, and integrated before we can progress toward spiritual enlightenment.

- Lord Shiva, who like the Crone is often called the destroyer, is also the one who purifies everyone with his name. Symbolically this is the part of us that is willing to eat away the flesh of our own creations, even the so-called poisonous aspects, in order to absorb what is good and to release the rest.

- The various precious objects that emerge from the ocean during the churning represent the psychic or spiritual powers (*siddhis*) that we gain as we progress spiritually from one stage to the next. The fact that the gods and goddesses are present to distribute gifts suggests that they know how easy it is for the seeker to be hampered by or in awe of these powers. This leads to a desire to possess them rather than to use them wisely for the good of all concerned. These divine beings help us maintain our focus by giving us only what we are capable of handling at any one time.

- Mohini the alluring temptress symbolizes the greatest challenges to the spiritual disciple: pride and self-magnification, which arise from a nonintegrated ego. It is only when we accept that pride maintains separation that we can bow our heads in humility and dive back into the unified field of the sea of milk to achieve the self-realization we seek.

- The amrita, or the elixir of immortality, is our ultimate achievement.
- The fact that it is only Rahu's head that becomes immortal speaks to the Hindu understanding of reincarnation. This says that the essential wisdom of our experiences will merge with the eternal sea of milk, while the untamed and poorly integrated parts of ourselves will return to earthly existence for further refinement.

This beautiful description of the path toward spiritual enlightenment or eternal life highlights the challenges and opportunities we all face at this particular time. Through our courage to find and embody all aspects of our essential self, we too have the opportunity to taste the elixir of life.

THE ELIXIR OF LIFE

What is this potent potion that is so highly prized throughout all traditions? It has many names, such as the already mentioned amrita (Indian), the fountain of life (Christian), the elixir of immortality, dancing water, ambrosia (Greek), pool of nectar, and the quintessence of life.

Alchemists throughout the ages have attempted to produce this elixir through chemical processes that combine the four elements of earth, air, fire, and water into the fifth element of ether. They believe that by consuming these white drops (liquid gold), good health, eternal youth, and immortality will result.

Others believe this magical potion is produced naturally by a woman's vagina during the act of sex and is then known as *the divine nectar of the sacred waters* containing the fountain of youth. Indeed, research has shown that a fluid, ejaculated from glands in the anterior vaginal walls, contains an enzyme that extends the life of cells and hence has been called *the enzyme of immortality*. However, there is no proof that if a man drinks this fluid during intercourse he will immediately experience immortality!

The true elixir of life is believed to be produced at the level of the crown chakra, from the pineal gland, by the careful development of our sexual serpentine ladder. Represented by the lily or the lotus, the elixir of life is linked strongly to the Dark Goddess Lilith. Like other crones, Lilith was instrumental in teaching her priestesses how to produce this fountain of youth through sacred sexual practices. Such priestesses would draw their partner up along their serpentine ladder during intercourse, allowing them to experience moments of orgasmic bliss as they bathed in her elixir of life.

It's interesting to note that Lilith was the first wife of Adam but he refused to see her as his equal and demanded that she should lie under him during sexual intercourse. Affronted by this suggestion, she abandoned Adam for the desert, leaving Adam to ask God for a substitute, Eve. This sounds as if Adam lost his opportunity for immortality due to one bad decision!

Hindu tradition also believes that amrita is produced from the pineal gland during deep states of meditation, when the serpentine kundalini energy rises up from the base chakra to the crown chakra, stimulating this tiny gland. Teachings profess that just one drop of this potent elixir is enough to conquer death. This same process is described by the Egyptian alchemists who described the release of amrita when the union takes place between the Djed and the Ba body, leading to the ignition of the Ka body.

The tale of Samudra Manthan reminds us of the stages we must pass through in order to produce our own elixir of life and enter our own light or Ka body. As the Ka grows, we will find ourselves less affected by the challenges of aging: looking younger and staying healthier. As we begin to live a more multidimensional existence, time will become less of an influential factor in our lives and we will come to understand the truth behind the word *time:* a Temporarily Induced Mind Experiment (TIME).

On this path toward the "now" of immortality, we naturally remember that, in truth, no separation has ever existed between us and the Heart of the Great Mother except through the limiting beliefs of our own mind.

The following personal story illustrates how limiting beliefs plus unhealthy doses of guilt and fear may keep us locked in a state of isolation from the Great Mother's unconditional love that is our birthright.

PAT'S STORY

Embraced by the Heart of the Great Mother

I was shown how subtly invasive religious dogmas can be when I attended the funeral of my dear friend Pat a few years ago. As the service proceeded, I watched with fascination as Pat's spirit danced around her coffin. She was commenting on its quality and proudly introducing me to her natural birth family, whom she had met only after passing from this Earth plane. On several occasions I had to stop myself from laughing out loud as Pat exuded the joy of a soul free from the restrictions of the physical body.

She even moved among the mourners, offering them words of encouragement and love, urging them not to grieve her passing but instead remember their happy times together. Then, as the Catholic priest began his sermon, weaving traditional doctrines with personal sentiments, she settled under the pulpit, concentrating hard on what he was saying and nodding occasionally—until he started to talk about sin and shame.

"Our dear sister Pat's sins have been forgiven, her shame has been washed clean, and she has been allowed to enter God's mansion," said the priest.

Immediately Pat's spirit became very animated and in a voice so loud I was sure everyone in the church could hear it, she exclaimed: "No, no, that's not the truth! The only shame is that I wasn't taught that I was always welcome in God's house! I now know it was only my beliefs sustained through guilt that caused me to feel unworthy and to maintain the separation for so long."

Turning to me, she looked directly into my eyes and said, "Never let the illusionary state of inadequacy get in the way of your true, eternal connection to the source. There is nothing you need to do or change to be accepted into the kingdom of heaven. This is not a place but a state of being in which your luminous self already resides, waiting for you to step over the threshold of uncertainty and remember who you really are."

6

THE ALCHEMICAL EMERALD TABLET

We cannot continue our exploration of immortality and our union with the Heart of the Great Mother without acknowledging the science of the mystics—alchemy—and its treatise, the Emerald Tablet. Alchemy can be a practical science where base metals are turned into gold or a profound spiritual journey where, through careful stages of initiation, we achieve the golden light of illumination; we become immortal.

Here is what the Count of St. Germain, a master alchemist born around 1560 CE, says about alchemy, often known as the Great Art: "The inner meaning of alchemy is simply all-composition, implying the relation of the all of the creation to the parts which compose it. Thus alchemy, when properly understood, deals with the conscious power of controlling mutations and transmutations within Matter and energy and even within life itself. It is the science of the mystic and the forte of the self-realized man who, having sought, has found himself to be one with God and is willing to play his part."[1]

St. Germain taught that self-mastery was the key to this Great Art in which the alchemist could, through his actions, determine the design of his own life's creation and hence fulfill his destiny. He warned any developing alchemist to be aware of self-delusion and rationalization.

For thousands of years alchemists have considered the Emerald

Tablet to be their bible. It is an ancient artifact said to contain advanced spiritual technology describing the steps required to achieve personal transformation and accelerated species evolution. Encompassing all levels at once—mind, body, and spirit—the tablet's teachings have threatened many who wish to maintain their dominance over the masses. The Emerald Tablet's message, however, is greater than the small minds of men, and through time its thrust has become enriched, translated, and revered, carrying its readers to ever-expanding levels of consciousness. Described as being molded out of a single piece of green crystal, it has caught the attention and imagination of many scholars, writers, and scientists, including Sir Isaac Newton and Carl Jung. Its origins are somewhat obscure although it is usually attributed to an author known as Hermes Trismegistus—but who was he?

HERMES TRISMEGISTUS

His name means "thrice greatest," which recognizes that as far as we know he incarnated three times. His human manifestations are as Thoth, Akhenaten, and Balinas.

Thoth

The First Hermes

The first Hermes has a very mixed heritage, combining history, mythology, and mysticism. According to mythology, his first appearance was as an immortal Atlantean priest-king ruling an ancient colony of Egypt from 50,000 to 36,000 BCE. Researcher Dr. M. Doreal hypothesizes that originally there were twelve emerald-green tablets formed from a substance created through alchemical transmutation, making them imperishable and unchangeable. Engraved into their surface were characters in an ancient Atlantean language, which responded to attuned thought waves imprinting the appropriate vibration directly into the mind of the reader. The tablets were apparently fastened together with hoops of golden-copper alloy and were suspended from a rod of the same material. Before he left this earth plane, Thoth combined the multiple

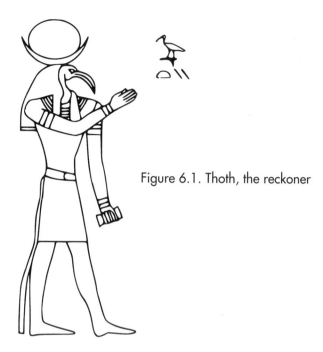

Figure 6.1. Thoth, the reckoner

tablets into one text—now known as the Emerald Tablet—and hid this artifact along with other ancient objects, texts, records, and instruments of Atlantis under the Great Pyramid.[2]

Thoth reappeared as an Egyptian deity and enjoyed popularity from 2670 to 2205 BCE when he was seen as the god of magic; inventor of writing (in particular, hieroglyphics); teacher of logic and speech; founder of mathematics, science, and medicine; and in essence, the representative of One Mind.[3]

In his other role, he was known as the revealer of the hidden, the lord of rebirth, and the great measurer or reckoner of the universe. As such, he was given the authority to judge the dead, weighing an individual's heart against a feather to assess how closely he or she had followed, through words and actions, the soul's innermost intent.

Akhenaten
The Second Hermes
The pharaoh Akhenaten, also known as Amenhotep IV, ruled from 1364 to 1347 BCE, setting up a monotheistic religion—much to the

displeasure of the priests who enjoyed the power brought by worship of many deities. Akhenaten espoused the concept of living in the pure essence of truth, where the sacred marriage between the will of the One Mind and the force of the One Thing opened a portal in our sun that showered rays of light or consciousness onto all of humanity from the Creative Source or Great Mother.[4]

Figure 6.2. Akhenaten, Nefertiti, and their children
with the solar disk

Photo of stone carving in Egyptian Museum in Berlin

Married to the beautiful Nefertiti, they often look extraterrestrial in appearance due to their elongated skulls. After seventeen years of reign, during which time many of the corrupt practices of the past were overturned, husband and wife both disappeared and their bodies were never found. They were replaced by the boy pharaoh Tutankhamen, and power quickly reverted back to the hands of the priests, although Egyptian supremacy was never the same again. Some surmise that Akhenaten was actually none other than Moses. If they actually were the same person then perhaps Akhenaten didn't die but instead carried his message and legacy out of Egypt and toward the Promised Land.[5]

If we follow this lead then perhaps Akhenaten did not receive the Emerald Tablet until, as the Bible states, Moses climbed Mount Sinai to communicate with God and hence receive the Ten Commandments for his people. The Lord said to Moses, "Come up to me on the mountain and wait there, that I may give you the tablets of stone, with the law and the commandment, which I have written for their instruction" (Exodus 24:12).

We then learn from the Bible (Exodus 32:19) that when Moses returns to the people, he finds they have created a golden calf in honor of the cow goddess Hathor. In his anger, he breaks the original tablets and returns to the mountain so that God can write a new set of commandments. Were these new commandments different from the first set due to the fact that God had decided humans were not ready to control their own lives?

The final twist at the end of this tale may provide the answers. According to the Bible (Exodus 32:20) Moses is told by God to cast the golden calf into a fierce fire to produce powdered gold, scatter it on water, and then give it to the people to drink. Could it be Moses created monoatomic or alchemical gold and, by giving it to the people, thereby altered their consciousness to move forward away from Egypt and into the new world? We may never know the truth.

Balinas (Also Known as Apollonius of Tyana)

The Third Hermes

The next time the tablet surfaces is in 332 BCE, when it is found in a temple in Siwa by Alexander the Great after his victory in Egypt. Immediately he translated the text into Greek and used its knowledge to enhance his power, success, and fortune. He hid the tablet for safekeeping but died during a journey to India. The tablet was found three centuries later by a youth called Balinas, who was born in 16 CE in what is now Turkey.[6]

Through appreciation and integration of the tablet's teachings, Balinas became a great mystic with wise and magical powers, especially in the field of healing. Unfortunately the followers of Christ were jealous of his powers, and by 400 CE many of Balinas's books and temples had been destroyed. His writings, however, were not completely lost, and in 650 CE *The Book of Balinas the Wise on Causes* appeared in Arabic.

ALCHEMICAL TRANSFORMATION

What follows is a modern translation of a portion of the Emerald Tablet summarizing how to produce the philosopher's stone or elixir of life in order to achieve immortality.

Following the entire translation, I have broken the treatise into sections and added my commentary on its meaning.

> *In truth, without deceit, certain, and most veritable.*
> *That which is Below corresponds to that which is Above*
>   *and*
> *that which is Above corresponds to that which is Below*
> *to accomplish the miracles of the One Thing.*
> *And just as all things have come from this One Thing*
>   *through the meditation of the One Mind,*
> *so do all created things originate from this One Thing,*
>   *through transformation.*

> *Its Father is the Sun, its Mother the Moon.*
> *The Wind carries it in its belly; its nurse is the Earth.*
> *It is the origin of All, the consecration of the Universe;*
>   *its inherent Strength is perfected, if it is turned into*
>   *Earth.*

Separate the Earth from Fire, the Subtle from the
    Gross,
gently and with great ingenuity.
It rises from earth to heaven and descends again to
    earth, thereby combining within Itself
the powers of both the Above and the Below.

Thus will you obtain the Glory of the Whole Universe.
All obscurity will be clear to you.
This is the greatest Force of powers because it overcomes
every Subtle thing and penetrates every Solid thing.

In this way was the Universe created.
From this comes many wondrous applications, because
    this is the Pattern.
Therefore am I called Thrice Greatest Hermes,
    having all three parts of the wisdom of the Whole
    Universe. Herein have I completely explained the
    Operation of the Sun.[7]

In truth, without deceit, certain, and most veritable.

Free of dogma, without ego, centered, and most intuitive. These few words set the scene for a profound experience; their study is, in itself, a lifetime's work. Simply stated, we are told that the process of alchemical transformation can occur only when we learn to:

- Be honest with our thoughts, words, and actions where nothing is hidden and everything is owned.
- Master (not suppress) our emotions and energies.
- Carry a level of self-confidence that has no need to judge others.
- Release our need to defend our opinions.
- Live from a place of discernment, detached from the outcome.

- Think, act, and speak from our central core, where head and heart are aligned.
- Be guided by our intuition, driven not by fear but by love.

That which is Below corresponds to that which is
  Above and
that which is Above corresponds to that which is Below
to accomplish the miracles of the One Thing.
And just as all things have come from this One Thing
  through the meditation of the One Mind,
so do all created things originate from this One Thing,
  through transformation.

This rubric reminds us that life is cyclical, with no true beginning or end, and that without such a continuum, alchemy cannot work. It also allows us to understand that both spirit and matter, the above and the below, demand equal reverence, for they exchange energy continually. Finally it confirms that when the One Mind, our attention, is clearly focused on the One Thing—dynamic creative potential or our imagination—then miracles will occur.

Its Father is the Sun, its Mother the Moon.
The Wind carries it in its belly; its nurse is the Earth.
It is the origin of All, the consecration of the Universe;
its inherent Strength is perfected, if it is turned into
  Earth.

Having set the scene, the process is now described in detail, starting with the four elements that to an alchemist are considered to be the Prima Materia, or First Matter. As you will see, an appreciation of the power of these elements was encoded into both tarot and simple playing cards.

Fire: inspiration, wands, clubs; calcination
Water: feeling and emotions, cups, hearts; dissolution
Air: thinking, swords, spades; separation
Earth: sensation, pentacles, diamonds; conjunction

The Element of Fire

Its Father is the Sun . . .   Calcination

This phase related to fire begins our journey.

From the text, we are asking the sun's heat to burn away—or calcinate—any beliefs, identities, or dogmas that do not align with the soul's deepest truth. These can be recognized by our need to defend them. If we fight for acknowledgment of our particular identity in the world or feel the need to convince people that what we believe is true, then these constructs come from the ego and not the soul. When our true identities are embraced by the heart, our inner light shines bright with the fire and passion of the soul and there is no need to defend anything.

Symbol: black bird and fires
Chakra: base, associated with security and stability
Element: fire

The Element of Water

. . . its Mother the Moon.   Dissolution

Now the ashes of calcination are scattered on the waters of the unconscious, further breaking down artificial constructs of the psyche, freeing the energy—often in the form of intense emotions—that has been trapped by a false sense of separation between our outer and inner lives, our personality and our soul. For those who have been well defended, this phase can be frightening. But the soul's presence gently persuades us to let go and trust, accepting the discomfort of not knowing who we are or where we are going.

As the emotions settle, a state of euphoria often emerges as we find ourselves floating in our own unconscious without the fears that have entrapped us for so long. Yet it is also important at this stage not to become lost in delusion, believing we have already reached the eagerly anticipated union with the Divine. The dissolution is just the beginning.

Symbol: black bird, water, mirrors, and tears
Chakra: sacral, associated with intimate relationships
Element: water

The Element of Air

The Wind carries it in its belly . . .   Separation

As we move into this phase, it is time to reclaim and integrate the dreams and golden insights from our soul that surfaced during dissolution. This invigorating fresh air encourages us to listen to our intuition and apply healthy filters, choosing beliefs that nurture our soul.

Over time we feel less burdened and increasingly self-confident, as if we have been given wings to fly. We also find that our ability to be objective and clear-sighted grows stronger, helping us to avoid the tricks and illusions that attempt to draw us back into our old patterns of behavior. Now we are ready to create a new reality based on the richness of our soul.

Symbol: black bird, air, and swords
Chakra: solar plexus, associated with self-confidence
Element: air

The Element of Earth

. . . its nurse is the Earth.   Conjunction

The Earth offers the vessel for the planting, nurturing, and blooming of our dreams as we commit to living our truth. This is a time for conjunction, or the sacred marriage of opposites, when spirit and soul meet and produce a fragile child called the *lesser stone*. This stage is often marked by an increase in psychic awareness accompanied by synchronicities as we reconnect to greater realms of consciousness. Many choose to stop at this point, happy with their spiritual successes as their psychic juices flow.

But the philosopher's stone waits in the darkness for those willing to commit to their own personal inner work.

Symbol: cockerel, lovers, weddings
Chakra: personal heart, associated with acceptance of duality
Element: earth

Separate the Earth from Fire, the Subtle from the Gross,
gently and with great ingenuity.

This stage, one of putrefaction and fermentation through fire, is the turning point in the Great Art. Commonly it envelops us in a dark night of the soul as we choose to go within and descend to meet the Dark Goddess and our own personal demons. At some point we step into her cauldron—the vessel used for the processes of putrefaction and fermentation—and find ourselves stewing in our own creative juices.

As more of the mental chatter, emotional manure, and illusionary insights are broken down, the fermentation process brings to the surface all of our subpersonalities, which require acceptance and integration. As each is brought out of the shadows and into the light we experience a strength and freedom that we might have previously believed to be unattainable.

For an alchemist the sign that putrefaction is reaching its end is the appearance of a white milky liquid on the surface of rotting material. This esoterically represents the white light of resurrection, proving that consciousness has survived the "death." Symbolically, this is represented by a White Swan, gliding across still waters that run deep, reflecting the fact that, despite the dark times, the inner light is always present.

The sign that fermentation is almost complete is seen in the formation of the Peacock's Tail, when an iridescent film of oil appears on the putrefying organic material. The eyes on the feathers represent the many aspects of the self now revealed.

Chemically, at the end of fermentation, an alchemist sees the production of a solid yellow ferment representing the final stages of the transformation of gold from the base material. This is known as the Golden Pill. This yellow waxy substance is the literal incarnation of thought and the first indication that we are making gold. It is formed from the union of inspiration above and imagination below (One Mind and One Thing) and is called the *secret fire*. It opens the portal to higher realms and multidimensional existence.

> **Symbol:** end of putrefaction, the white swan; end of fermentation, the peacock tail
>
> **Chakras:** throat chakra, the willingness to enter the cauldron

*It rises from earth to heaven and descends again to
earth, thereby combining within Itself
the powers of both the Above and the Below.*

Through the process of distillation, the soup containing our subpersonalities plus the emotions that kept our stories alive is continually heated and cooled until only the pure essence of each character remains. This essence or wisdom is then fed to the heart, enhancing its perpetual fire and causing the Ka to brighten.[8]

Symbol: distillation is represented by the pelican, which feeds its young with its own blood—our ability to feed ourselves with the light of consciousness from our experiences

Chakra: heart and third eye, acting through detached compassion

Thus will you obtain the Glory of the Whole Universe.
All obscurity will be clear to you.
This is the greatest Force of powers because it overcomes
every Subtle thing and penetrates every Solid thing.

Coagulation occurs when the distilled essence rises up to meet the essential self or Ba, and the second sacred marriage occurs to give meaning to the phrase *I am that I am.* Once this stage is reached, we know the freedom of spirit that can move with ease between the dimensions. For the alchemist, this mobile state of consciousness is the *philosopher's stone,* also known as the *elixir of life.*

Symbol: the phoenix

Chakra: third eye and crown chakra, living in the oneness of truth, wisdom, and love

In this way was the Universe created.
From this comes many wondrous applications, because
this is the Pattern.

This pattern is available to everybody.

Therefore am I called Thrice Greatest Hermes,
having all three parts of the wisdom of the Whole
Universe. Herein have I completely explained the
Operation of the Sun.

This explains the principal forces that are essential for the process of alchemy and enlightenment symbolized in the Trinity. The same message is reflected in the intimate relationship between the Virgin, Mother, and Crone: the glorious aspects that together form the heart of the Great Mother.

PART TWO

The Celestial Design

In part 2, we'll look skyward and explore how the movements of the celestial bodies, especially the moon, reflect our own inner search for enlightenment and immortality.

7

RHYTHMS OF THE MOON

Of all the planets, stars, and astronomical bodies in the sky, it is the Earth's satellite—our moon—that most closely exemplifies the cyclic nature of creation. Its precise harmonious orbits around Mother Earth reflect the pure compassion that exists between the Great Mother and us, her much beloved creations.

CHARACTERISTICS OF THE MOON

The Moon's Impact on Our Psyche

Despite the "one giant leap for mankind" taken in 1969, there is still so much we do not know or understand about the moon's mysteries, especially when it comes to its effect on our psyche. Even though some may poke fun at those who allude to an association between human behavior and the moon, who hasn't been awestruck by the vision of a full orange ball rising above the horizon at sunset or by the first sighting of the crescent moon in the dark sky? Unlike its solar equivalent, this heavenly mass appears to have no obvious purpose and yet is inherently revered by all.

It is well-known that the moon's silvery sheen is due entirely to the reflected light of the sun. Subsequently, it offers a pure and perfect mirror for anything projected upon it, which is why the moon has been used as a focus for all our projected psychological shadows, reflecting whatever is in our deep unconscious. Some individuals sense mystery, others a joyful familiarity, and a few the face of madness.

Our psychological relationship to the moon is expressed in words such as *lunacy,* from the Latin word for the moon, *luna,* and *mental,* from *mens,* meaning "a lunar month." Historically such terms were meant to represent an ecstatic union between us and this heavenly body but they have become distorted, often reflecting a psychiatric disorder rather than a state of heavenly bliss. The root *mens* also gives us *menses, menstrual,* and *menopause* because of the strong link between a woman's creative rhythms, the moon's phases, and how she feels at certain times in her life.

In past decades, space exploration to the moon has played a major role in shifting the consciousness of humankind. When the first images appeared of the Earth rising over the horizon of the moon during the Apollo voyages, we somehow knew we were no longer alone in the universe. At the same time, many of us fell in love with this fragile, blue globe, the Earth, heightening our awareness of the honored position we hold as its guests—a fact we seem to keep forgetting.

Moon Gods and Goddesses

As the moon is commonly represented as having a feminine nature, you may be surprised to learn that a study of world history reveals that both moon gods and moon goddesses were often worshipped simultaneously. Indeed, in many early cultures it was the moon god (not the goddess) who conferred fertility and nurturance, with women and farmers praying to this deity for fruitful abundance.

One such moon god was Nanna from ancient Sumer, a civilization established around 5000 BCE in Southern Mesopotamia, south of modern Baghdad. Symbolized by a crescent moon, Nanna was seen as the torch of the night illuminating primeval darkness as he constantly renewed himself like a snake.

He taught the people there was a perfect time for everything and that when we flow with these cycles, life becomes easier. Thus he ruled tidal waters, human emotions, the fertility of crops, the endocrine system, and, of course, the menstrual cycle, which so closely follows the cosmic cycle of creativity. Without these cycles, the ancient people knew their land and lives would become dry and barren. It's a shame that Nanna isn't here today to remind us of the folly of trying to control such important cyclical events as menopause, menses, sleep cycles, and the timing of birth and death.

Following Nanna's guidance, our Sumerian ancestors lived by these rhythms. They saw the waxing or crescent moon as the most propitious time to fertilize crops, ideas, and people; the word *crescent* coming from the Latin *creare* meaning "to create." During a waning moon, harvesting and pruning took place, allowing the old to die, and compost to be created for new growth. Nobody would think of planting crops or starting a new business during this time. Those who lived close to the tidal waters had their own ideas, believing that a good birth was one connected to an incoming tide, whereas to die "well" was to expire as the tide went out.

I wonder how our health and productivity would be transformed if we adopted these rhythms, both in our personal lives and in the arenas of commerce, medicine, and education. It was only with the transition from lunar to solar worship approximately three thousand years ago that there was a distinct emergence of a moon goddess. The priests of the day, eager to distance themselves from anything feminine, portrayed this moon goddess as a fearful goddess of death, which totally ignored her beauty and natural rhythms. One such moon goddess is Artemis, often depicted as a dispassionate nighttime huntress carrying her bow (the crescent moon), accompanied by her faithful hunting dogs. This same stereotype is repeated in Mexican mythology in which the moon goddess is seen as a demon roaming the skies at night, seeking victims to devour. Indeed, many funerary traditions even today include the practice of adorning those who have died with crescent-shaped amulets in the hope of ensuring favor from the moon goddess as the journey through the realms of death begins.

The Moon and the Elixir of Life

Who would have thought the unassuming moon would have such a strong connection to the secret of immortality? In fact many traditions offer rich descriptions of their moon gods and goddesses involved in alchemy.

Take for instance Chandra, a Hindu moon god who, dressed in white, carries a crescent moon–shaped bow. He is seen as the guardian of soma, the nectar of immortality. This precious elixir is fermented from the milky white juice of a plant that grows exclusively upon his sacred mountains.

This association between moon deities and mountains is a common theme probably because our ancestors believed that mountains act as lightning rods between heaven and earth. They believed optimal times for the transmission of consciousness occurred when the sun and moon were aligned as perfect dancing partners.

As we shall see later, this belief caused our ancestors to emulate the shape and strength of mountains, by building towers, pyramids, and ziggurats to act as transformers, converting spirit into matter and matter into spirit.

Our next link between the moon and the elixir of immortality comes from China, where moon cakes are still served at a festival that falls on the fifteenth day of the eighth moon of the Chinese year. This date equates to the September equinox and to what is known as the Harvest Moon, a time of abundance and prosperity.

This ancient tradition from China invites us to meet Chang'e, a beautiful female immortal being who comes to Earth to help her people. The next part of the account varies depending upon the version, although all agree that Chang'e eventually swallows a pill or magic potion that contains the elixir of life and finds herself floating up to the moon where she becomes the moon goddess.

Her companion on the moon is a character who appears in many lunar legends, especially those originating in Asia, Central America, and the Australian continent. While those of us who live in Europe and North America see the dark troughs on the moon's surface as the "man in the moon," individuals in other parts of the world are convinced that the figure is a rabbit. Chang'e's assistant is known as *the jade rabbit* and this is his story:

Three fairy sages transform themselves into pitiful old men and beg for something to eat from a fox, a monkey, and a rabbit. The fox and the monkey both give food to the old men, but the rabbit, being empty-handed, jumps into the blazing fire, offering his own flesh for the men to eat. The sages are so touched by the rabbit's sacrifice that they let him live in the moon palace, where he is given the honored position of grinding the jade elixir of immortality.

This simple story carries an important message: through the sacrifice of our flesh (our earthly attachments) in the fiery cauldron of the Crone, we receive the promise of eternal life.

MOON WISDOM

Throughout history, people have been in awe of the moon, aware of how its ever-changing nature mirrors our own lives. Indeed, every night the Earth's constant companion is encoding us with messages that encourage us to embrace cycles of growth and transformation, develop healthy, interdependent relationships, and remember our own eternal nature.

Let's explore some of these insights now.

The Moon's Dance of Love

One of the most powerful messages the moon offers is the exquisite dance between darkness and light. In traditional teachings, the darkness of the moon is female—the mother energy—while the light is her son. During the dark moon days around the new moon, the mother is fully in her power, savoring the profound connection she makes with the Great Mother during this time. Then, as the moon begins to wax, we see a sliver of light as she gives birth to her son. The light of the moon becomes brighter, as the mother nurtures her son and the darkness decreases. Eventually at the full moon, all we see is light. At this time it could be said that the darkness—the mother—has sacrificed herself so that the light—her son—may become king. Then, within hours, a small sliver of darkness appears, and over time the light is consumed by the darkness until it is seen no more.

This theme of sacrifice in the name of love is played out in many myths in which the nurturing mother dies as her puer-hero-son leaves home to find his fortune. However, the second part of the story is rarely told: The son returns home as king and willingly feeds his mother with the seeds of his endeavors until he dies. His final act is to inseminate his mother with his seed so that at the new moon she will give birth to his son and heir.

This is the true nature of any reciprocally rewarding relationship in which both aspects of the cycle are willing to give and receive so each may flourish.

The Moon Tree

In some cultures, the symbol of a healthy relationship is represented by a sacred moon tree, which is protected by two winged animals. The lion is seen as a symbol of the interplay between dark and light while the unicorn is the symbol of unity and immortality. Together these animals reflect the paradox of divine creation: the lion represents the dynamic flow and tension between two opposite poles of existence—masculine and feminine or yin and yang—while the unicorn reflects the nurturing central, eternal energy, the original source of the duality. This is the true meaning of the trinity: the dynamic interplay of two opposing forces around a central core of eternal energy, the Heart of the Great Mother.

The profound symbolism portrayed by the moon tree is sung in hymns to Ishtar, the great Babylonian moon goddess, daughter of the moon god Sin. She is known as *the sacred tree* and embraces Tammuz, her consort and son. It is through his journey around her trunk that he comes to embody the light and dark aspects of the self. He is the new green growth, the full bloom of the flower, the luscious fruit, the precious seeds, and the compost, all of which represent the continuity of life. Their close interdependence is captured in the deep understanding that he must fertilize her with his seed when acting as her spouse, and in turn she will continually give birth to him in the form of her son.

It's interesting to note that in many moon-based cultures the felling of a tree is an important ritual signifying the willing sacrifice of the dying king to the Great Mother. Indeed, for the Egyptian god Osiris, a truncated tree was the resting place of his coffin. As such, it represented both the tomb and womb of the mother who lovingly embraces her dying consort who must die so she can give birth to his son. The tradition of cutting down a tree at Christmas and decking it with lights and baubles signifies both the death of the old king and the welcome of the new sun or son.

This healthy, symbiotic relationship reminds us of the interplay of energies that must exist within us for the production of the elixir of life. When two opposite poles of existence, such as our own masculine and feminine aspects, work together in perfect synergy and harmony, the result is a self-perpetuating flow of energy that has no end. As we shall see later, this specific movement of energy is represented by a sacred geometrical shape known as the toroid, which is found in many places including the womb, the heart, and the magnetic field around the Earth.

The Moon's "Dark Side"

You may have heard there's a "dark side" of the moon; it would be more accurate to say it has a hidden side. We all know the Earth travels around the sun and the moon travels around the Earth. Yet it is incredible that the rotations of the Earth and moon on their axes are in such perfect symmetry that we only ever see the same face of the moon; the opposite face is hidden permanently from us here on Earth. It was not until 1959 that the Luna 3 probe exposed the secrets of the moon's hidden face showing a deeply potholed and mountainous terrain.

Could this hidden side of the moon reflect the "hidden" side of us, only to be seen with our inner eyes?

Dark Nights of the Moon

Nearly all traditions agree that the process of death and rebirth—transformation—requires at least three days, symbolic of the three dark moon nights before the light of the moon returns to the sky. It is therefore inexplicable that the Christian festival of Easter, which represents the death and resurrection of Jesus, is in fact positioned to take place at the time of a full moon and not a new moon. We can only imagine how the effectiveness of the Easter message has been diminished by this distortion. The cover-up is more significant when we see that the all-important messages of renewal and resurrection—the miraculous ignition of Jesus's Ka—is represented by yellow bunnies and chocolate eggs.

FOLLOWING THE MOON PHASES FOR HEALTH AND ABUNDANCE

There can be few people who haven't been impressed by the changing faces of the moon in the night sky, even in the most light-polluted environments. Yet outside traditional cultures, it is seldom taught that each moon phase represents a different phase of the hero's journey toward spiritual enlightenment.

Each month, with the help of the moon's energy, we are encouraged to plant and nurture our dreams, celebrate our successes, harvest the fruits of our endeavors, and allow compost to form so that new ideas can be born. If we can plan our lives to correspond to the unique features of each phase of the moon, life will flow with far greater ease. Perhaps you'd like to mark the new moon in your diary (it's often depicted as a dark circle) and follow the instructions below while watching your emotions, thoughts, and energy change with each of the moon's phases.

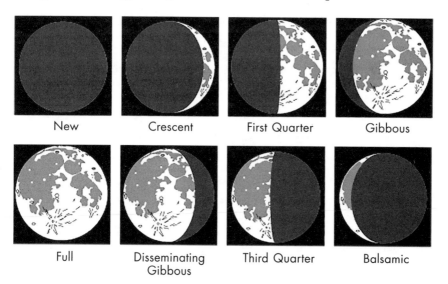

| New | Crescent | First Quarter | Gibbous |

| Full | Disseminating Gibbous | Third Quarter | Balsamic |

Figure 7.1. The phases of the moon

The phases of the moon are described in the following ways:

New Moon Phase: Up to 3½ days after the new moon

Impulse: to germinate and emerge

Archetype: puer or boy-child

Action: This is a time to eagerly plant new seeds of inspiration or begin a new project. Even though the final manifestation of these seeds may be unclear, there is an instinctual urge to commit to these dreams or ideas so they will eventually see the light of day.

....

Crescent Moon Phase: 3½–7 days after the new moon

Impulse: to move forward through focused attention

Archetype: puer to hero

Action: As the desire to propel our dreams into the light of consciousness continues there is often an opposing force that seeks security and comfort in what is already known. We can find ourselves making excuses why we need to stay small, why our projects won't work, or why we need more information before moving forward. Through focused attention we come to recognize that any struggles, whether internal or external, are merely the means of strengthening our spiritual muscle or resolve.

....

First Quarter Phase: 7–10½ days after the new moon

Impulse: to build and decide

Archetype: hero

Action: At this point there is a strong determination to redefine our goals so we can experience personal success. This causes us to examine and release old beliefs and patterns of limited thinking that could prevent our dreams becoming reality.

....

Waxing Gibbous Moon Phase: 10½–14 days after the new moon

Impulse: to improve and perfect

Archetype: hero to king

Action: Now, as we approach the spotlight of the full moon, we are both excited and perhaps nervous. Are we ready for the world to see who we are, and how will they judge our manifested dreams? In the end perfection is not a future goal but a state of contentment that exists in the present moment.

....

Full Moon Phase: 15–18½ days after the new moon

Impulse: to achieve success and full expression of the ego

Archetype: king

Action: This is a moment to celebrate, allowing everybody to see the full bloom of our success. Yet the festivities may be delayed if we keep looking outside ourselves for approval. The full moon allows us to shine in the spotlight of our true light.

....

Waning Gibbous or Disseminating Moon Phase: 3½–7 days after the full moon

Impulse: to disseminate information

Archetype: lover

Action: Here we are given the opportunity to fertilize our manifested dreams as we share our experiences with others through social networking, talking, and teaching. It's important to walk our talk and then realize there is a fundamental difference between personal or ego success and soul fulfillment.

....

Last or Third Quarter Moon Phase: 7–10½ days after the full moon

Impulse: to revise and reevaluate

Archetype: sage

Action: After all the excitement it's time for an honest review: Did the end product match our initial dream or idea? What gems of wisdom can we take from the experience? What did we learn about ourselves and what may we need to change next month? As a time of reevaluation, it's not a good time to start something new.

....

Balsamic Moon Phase: 10½ days after the full moon
and until the new moon

Impulse: to distill and transform

Archetype: magician

Action: As this particular cycle comes to its close, we'll often seek periods of solitude as we distill the seeds of wisdom from the rest of the story, offering them back to the Great Mother to enrich her consciousness. As we release our hold on the emotions and expectations from this recent project, we can gracefully surrender to the love of the Great Mother, becoming one, once again, with her ocean of possibilities. We've reached the stage of soul fulfillment.

....

Dark Moon Phase: 3 days around the new moon
(day 2 is the new moon)

Impulse: to float in the ocean of potential and no-thingness

Archetype: Great Mother's primordial waters

Action: Now we enter three days of darkness—the dark moon days—when the moon is conjunct the sun and the illuminated face of the moon is hidden from the earth. This is a time to rest and recuperate as you reconnect with your soul's essence and the spiritual beings who love you unconditionally and who act as constant and wise companions on your path. Then on day three, something begins to stir again within the dark waters of the Great Mother and you're inspired with new dreams and ideas. A new cycle begins.

Each of us was born within a particular phase of the moon, calculated by assessing the position of our natal moon in relationship to our natal sun. This can be located by looking at the astrological birth chart and reveals the particular emphasis of our spiritual journey in this lifetime.

THE LUNATION PHASES

The famous astrologer Dane Rudhyar first examined the lunation phases and recognized that the phase of the moon under which each of us is born is an accurate indicator of both our core personality type and our life purpose. He came to this conclusion through a close study of the interaction between the solar outer consciousness and the instinctual nature of lunar awareness.[1]

It follows naturally that when the moon transits its natal position, we become highly sensitized to our purpose and are probably more focused on this than at any other time in the month. It is also a time when specific challenges linked to our particular phase of the creative cycle will arise, giving us the opportunity to overcome them in the most propitious way possible.

In the 1950s, Czech psychiatrist Dr. Eugene Jonas discovered it was not uncommon for a woman to be most fertile during the lunation phase of her natal chart, often causing her to experience spontaneous ovulation. This explains why some women become pregnant at times that are outside their menstrual midpoint, an important factor to be taken into account both in terms of infertility and the efficacy of the natural methods of contraception.[2]

What Phase Was I Born In?

I am grateful to Demetra George for her deep understanding of these lunar phases.[3] To calculate your own lunation phase, you first need to identify the sign and degree of your sun and moon in your natal chart.*

As an example, let's use the following settings from figure 7.2 on page 112: the sun at 6 degrees Virgo and the moon at 4 degrees Cancer.

Starting at the sun, walk around the astrology chart counterclockwise (anticlockwise), counting the number of degrees separating the sun from the moon while remembering that each sign consists of 30 degrees.

---

*One good place to get a free natal astrology chart is Astro.com. For an easy calculation of your particular lunation phase you can visit the Astrocal website.

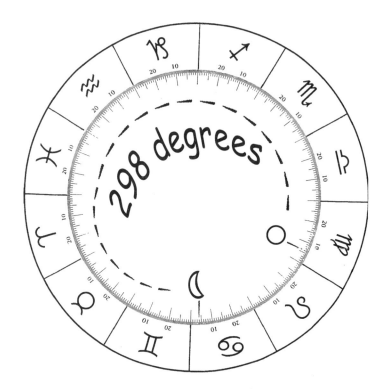

Figure 7.2. Calculating the Lunation Phase

In this case, the moon is 298 degrees ahead of the sun and falls within the last or third quarter moon phase

Once you've calculated your lunation phase, the insights below will help you appreciate your specific strengths and challenges as well as to understand your all-important life purpose.

New Moon Phase

Time: up to 3½ days after the new moon
Degree: 0–45 degrees ahead of the sun
Life Purpose: to germinate and emerge

This phase begins a whole new cycle of creativity. Insight has been received and the seed of an idea has been planted but it is still germinating in the dark.

Those born into this lunation phase often have little awareness or wisdom from past experiences, causing them to work best through spontaneity and instinct. The intuitive forces that drive them arise from deep within their soul, causing their actions to often appear irrational to others. But their innocence and childlike enthusiasm is so charming and irresistible that others will follow in their wake without knowing why.

Without conscious awareness of their purpose and direction but trusting their instincts, they can feel disconnected from the Earth. They are helped by becoming more present and aware of their bodies, by rooting themselves into Mother Earth, and by making a mark upon the world without seeking the approval of others to give them security.

Crescent Moon Phase

Time: 3½–7 days after the new moon
Degree: 45–90 degrees ahead of the sun
Life Purpose: to move and focus

The seedling now forces itself toward the light, challenged by an opposing force of gravity to stay within the comfort of the darkness.

Individuals born in this phase will find that, as they strive to express their uniqueness, limiting beliefs and fears from their past—especially from their childhood—emerge, creating tensions that may cause them to fall back into the relative comfort of failure and inertia. In addition, they are more susceptible to the emotional manipulation of others due to their poorly developed ego boundaries. Therefore, it's important to find ways to "thicken the stem"—the ego—in order to be able to overcome ancestral and personal fears and insecurities.

With determined focus, the excitement at the prospect of new growth drives them forward even though there may be occasional setbacks. These should be seen less as signs to withdraw and more as tools to strengthen the will. Through time, self-reliance develops as the soul identity of the individual starts to take root.

First Quarter Phase

Time: 7–10½ days after the new moon
Degree: 90–135 degrees ahead of the sun
Life Purpose: to build and decide

Now there is a strong determination to define goals and seek self-individuation.

With the moon square the sun, tension increases, compelling individuals born within this lunation phase to consciously choose to follow their own soul's path and build beliefs, identities, and relationships that nurture and protect their growth. Many challenges will be met along the way as old patterns present themselves to be cleared once and for all. For this to happen, clear and objective choices and decisions will need to be made from the stance of the hero rather from that of the victim.

Commonly, individuals born in this phase find that spiritual growth occurs through drama, conflict, and stress. They may even attract other people's problems into their lives or find themselves working in crisis situations. They are passionate and easily fired up by a challenge but need to learn how to manage stress skillfully by making wise decisions and managing chaos constructively and even objectively, rather than contributing to the problem.

As they learn to manage their own needs and energies, a healthy realization of their dreams and ideas continues.

Waxing Gibbous Moon Phase

Time: 10½–14 days after the new moon
Degree: 135–180 degrees ahead of the sun
Life Purpose: to improve and perfect

As the moon moves farther from the sun, self-confidence and self-actualization increase. There is an impetus to assess and refine the situation to produce the perfect bloom.

Those born within this lunation phase are gifted with the potential for great success but may be handicapped by self-doubt and self-criticism. Such individuals often feel they are "never good enough" and have difficulty breaking free of the rigid views they have of themselves and others.

Always attempting to "get it right," they find themselves over-analyzing situations rather than using that same keen insight to access, refine, and move ahead. Old patterns of resistance surface in order to be acknowledged and transformed; flexibility and objectivity are the keys to success. At this point, the light of the moon is much brighter. This, however, may be both a blessing and a curse, for now there are few places to hide and more pressure on them to fulfill their destiny.

Full Moon Phase

Time: 15–18½ days after the new moon
Degree: 180–225 degrees ahead of the sun
Life purpose: conscious integration and success

Here the sun and moon oppose each other; the sun representing the outer expressed consciousness—the ego or personality—and the moon the source of creative dreams, the soul.

Those individuals born during this phase soon learn that both poles of existence need to be equally honored and respected—the soul and the personality—to know true success. Without conscious acceptance of both, conflict arises, preventing either aspect from reaching the peak of achievement.

For these individuals, this same dynamic may play out in relationships where they seek someone to make them whole such as "the perfect match or soul mate." If such a mate is not found, they may focus their attention on a guru, teacher, or a group in order to become complete. Eventually, it is hoped, they will see the light and realize that the sacred marriage they seek is not to be found in another person, but instead involves the synthesis of their own inner polarities, especially those between thought and action, spirit and matter, and soul and personality.

As they consciously accept and integrate these polarities, their intention becomes embodied in reality and their life becomes full. They can stand tall like a rose in full bloom.

Waning Gibbous or Disseminating Moon Phase

Time: 3½–7 days after the full moon
Degree: 225–270 degrees ahead of the sun
Life Purpose: to distribute and convey

After standing in its own light and knowing what it is like to be fully alive, the light of the moon begins to wane.

For those born in this phase, this is a time to both enjoy the fruits of their endeavors and offer the insights they have gained to others. Thus, this is a life of disseminating the wisdom gleaned from lifetimes of experiences through teaching and writing, while always remembering the greatest teacher is someone who embodies the wisdom. It is therefore essential that those with this placement "walk their talk." If they do not, the message is empty and the words have no meaning, leading to low audience numbers and discontent on the part of the messenger. At times like this it's good to take time to regroup and reconnect to the inner teacher and ask: Do I believe in my own message? Another problem that can emerge is fanaticism: the mission to convey information and for others to accept their teachings becomes personal and objectivity is lost.

Ultimately these individuals will find the contentment they seek through their willingness to share ideas and thoughts with others—especially around global social issues—without attachment to a specific result.

Last or Third Quarter Moon Phase

Time: 7–10½ days after the full moon
Degree: 270–315 degrees ahead of the sun
Life Purpose: to revise and reevaluate

The seedling, having passed through magnificent bloom at full moon, now appears as lush fruit, full of wisdom gained through its courageous journey.

Individuals born in this lunation phase will find themselves constantly examining their beliefs in light of their experiences and asking: What is true? This mental scrutiny often sparks a crisis in consciousness, which can lead to several soul-searching events throughout the life of that individual. Their inner urges will force them to disengage from belief systems that are redundant, despite the coercion of others who have become dependent on the old familiar ways.

During this fermentation process, these individuals can be thrown into inner turmoil as the old paradigm dies and there is no obvious successor. Coupled with this, they may be unable to share with others what they are going through for fear of inciting disappointment and judgment. Subsequently, they may try to hide the changes that are occurring deep within. But it's important for them to understand that the profound changes taking place in their own thought processes will positively benefit not only their lives but also the lives of generations to come, stretching far beyond their immediate family.

To survive this metamorphosis, it's vital not to throw the baby out with the bath water. Instead, honor what has been learned and refined through many lifetimes and remember this will very soon become compost for future seeds of inspiration.

Balsamic Moon Phase

Time: 10½ days after full moon until the new moon
Degree: 315–360 degrees ahead of the sun
Life Purpose: to distill and transform

The last light of the inverted crescent moon eventually fades and darkness prevails as the developed seed containing the distilled essence of experience falls from the parent plant and lies dormant in the earth, awaiting germination.

Those born within this dark lunation phase will find their life embroiled with mystery, death, healing powers, and transformation. It is here the moon goddess rejoins her sun god to achieve soul fulfillment. For these individuals, their world straddles the old and the new. Much effort is spent completing unresolved issues, which often leads to intense, short-lived relationships. From early on, they may feel like outsiders to their family and peers, unable to connect to the ways of the past and unaware of any who speak their language as pioneers of new ideals.

Their inner sense of purpose causes them to focus all their attention on their prophetic and futuristic visions so their life will not be wasted. They often seek out a student—their metaphorical son and heir—to carry forward their ideas even at their own personal sacrifice.

This is one of the most complex lunation phases and completes the creative cycle until once again the seed is ready for germination and the new moon starts to form.

8

THE GREAT MOTHER'S
CELESTIAL ALCHEMY

As we expand our vision out into our galaxy, the Milky Way, we see that nothing is static in the sky above; each celestial body moves in perfect harmony with others. Even before the invention of the telescope, our ancestral architects knew about these graceful movements and built their sacred monuments to invite cosmic energies to enter Mother Earth during times of optimal alignment with these celestial bodies.

SOLAR AND LUNAR ECLIPSES

All ancient astronomers understood how the appearance of an eclipse could influence world history and were able to predict the timing of their appearance with great accuracy. Unscrupulous leaders would use this prior knowledge to trick their gullible populace into believing that it was through their power that the light of the sun and moon were extinguished for a few minutes.

An eclipse exists due to a specific alignment between the sun, moon, and Earth. A solar eclipse always occurs at the time of a new moon, when the moon, sitting between the sun and Earth, appears to completely cover the face of the sun, blocking its light.

A lunar eclipse, on the other hand, accompanies a full moon, with the Earth positioned between the sun and the moon preventing the sun's direct rays from reaching the moon's surface so that the moon appears dark. Solar and lunar eclipses always accompany each other fourteen days apart, although which appears first is dependent upon the orbital patterns of the sun and moon at that time. During a lunar eclipse the moon often appears blood red due to only the shorter wavelengths of the sun's light being able to pass through Earth's atmosphere to color the moon's surface. But this sinister hue often caused our ancestors to believe that a lunar eclipse was the devil inflicting terror on humanity as a punishment for wrongdoings.

Eclipse Mythology

Of the two types of eclipses, a lunar eclipse is more commonly associated with malevolence and mystery. Many cultures believe that during an eclipse the moon is swallowed by a mythological creature. To the Maya the jaguar was the culprit. To the Chinese the aggressor was a three-legged toad. And for others the culprit was a dragon. Whatever the beast accused of the crime, an eclipse brought with it a profusion of bad tidings. Indeed, it was not uncommon for citizens to run through the streets shouting, screaming, and banging drums to frighten away the evil spirits.

To the ancient Maya, the jaguar ruled the night; its spotted pelt represented the starry sky.[1] During a lunar eclipse, it was believed the jaguar's mouth was wide open, enticing individuals to enter the underworld and face those parts of themselves waiting within the darkness. This same belief is subconsciously held by people today who understand that during a lunar eclipse the glow of the full moon—our outer expression in the world—is shrouded, leaving us to face aspects of our psyche that live in the shadows. This causes dismay to some and ecstasy to others.

In the Hindu tradition, Rahu, a power-seeking demon depicted as having the head of a dragon and the body of a snake, swallows the sun or the moon, causing an eclipse. As we saw in the legend Samudra Manthan, Rahu, disguised as a god, manages to drink some of the amrita. But before this elixir of life can pass through his throat, Mohini cuts off Rahu's head, causing his body to remain untamed and unruly (symbolized by the serpent) while his head becomes immortal (the dragon). Traditionally, the head of this great demon is called Rahu and the tail is known as Ketu.

This myth offers us a further glimpse into the deeper mystery of an eclipse. It suggests that during such an event we are being offered the chance to partake of the drink of immortality. However, we may only do this after we have mastered our erratic serpentine energies, a practice deeply ingrained in the alchemical process of self-realization and the journey we're about to undertake.

We might assume that every time the moon passes behind the Earth, a lunar eclipse occurs. Yet the moon's orbit around the Earth

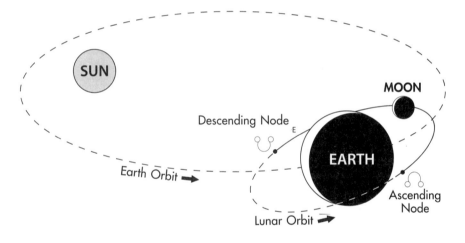

Figure 8.1. The north and south nodes of the moon
Image by Sherrie Frank

does not exactly follow the Earth's orbit around the sun on what is known as *the ecliptic plane*. This plane is the projection of the Earth's orbit onto the celestial sphere and marks the annual path of the sun. Twice a month the moon intersects this invisible ecliptic plane at virtual points known as the moon's nodes. When descending (Ketu), the point is known as the south node, and when ascending (Rahu), it is the north node.

Finding Our Own Nodes of the Moon

Within our natal astrological chart, each of us possess a north node and south node of the moon. Let's look at the moon's nodes as they relate to each of us as individuals, recognizing there are different schools of thought as to their interpretation. I'm offering one expanded upon by astrologer Jan Spiller that talks about the south node as our karma, or those things we're leaving behind, and the north node as our dharma, or those things we're embracing as our soul's destiny.[2] I also like to view the south node as what I am offering to the community from the wisdom of past experiences and the north node as what I am growing into or learning for myself as an individual.

Let's not assume the south node is negative but rather that its gifts are well-worn. As I like to say, "Just because you do something well, it doesn't mean you should keep doing it." The gifts of the north node are so new that we may just see them as a dream, not immediately recognizing that they belong to us. It takes courage to fully embody the qualities of one's north node—but believe me, the risk is worth taking.

The pressure from these two nodes for us to move forward never slackens. The south node acts as the bow and the north as the arrow, directing us toward our soul's potential. The moon's nodes are aided by the Virgin and Crone; the former acting as an intuitive guide urging us forward, the latter destroying old beliefs that would trap us in karmic patterns.

The following information is offered as a guide for you to understand your own journey through life, remembering that the placement of your south node indicates your past karma and what you are leaving behind and the north node represents your soul's purpose in this lifetime and beyond.*

---

*To find the placements of your nodes, one good place to access your natal astrological chart is Astro.com in the Horoscope Chart Drawings section. Here the north node is described as True Node and looks like a headset. The south node is in the sign opposite the north node and looks like a bucket handle.

Aries North Node, Libra South Node

Develop: independence, self-awareness, trusting your own impulses, courage, and the willingness to take risks

Leave behind: selflessness, being too nice, seeking the opinions of others, obsession with fairness, codependency, and the need to find an ideal, committed partnership

....

Taurus North Node, Scorpio South Node

Develop: loyalty, boundaries, patience, kindness, the ability to value your own gifts and talents, forgiveness, and an enjoyment of the senses

Leave behind: attraction to crisis situations, impatience, other people's business, intensity, overreacting, and brooding

....

Gemini North Node, Sagittarius South Node

Develop: curiosity, tact, logical thinking, asking what others think rather than assuming to know, seeing both sides of a situation, detachment

Leave behind: the need to be right, impatience, thinking you know what people are thinking without listening, careless spontaneity, taking shortcuts, and restlessness

....

Cancer North Node, Capricorn South Node

Develop: noticing and validating feelings, empathy, nurturing self, humility, and self-care

Leave behind: the need to be in control of everything, an excessive focus on goals, over responsibility for others, pessimism, and hiding feelings

....

Leo North Node, Aquarius South Node

Develop: individuality, a willingness to take center stage, following the heart's desires, strengthened willpower, enjoying life, and allowing the inner child to play

Leave behind: detachment, aloofness, waiting for others to prompt actions, waiting for knowledge before moving, and the need to always be different or rebel

....

Virgo North Node, Pisces South Node

Develop: participation, bringing order from chaos, the creation of routines, setting boundaries, self-contemplation, service to others, and the enjoyment of aesthetic beauty

Leave behind: being a victim, confusion, avoidance of making plans, escapism—especially into addictions and obsessions, day-dreaming, self-doubt, and self-delusion

....

Libra North Node, Aries South Node

Develop: cooperation, diplomacy, awareness of the needs of others, win-win situations, sharing, and selflessness

Leave behind: impulsiveness, self-assertion, poor judgment, self-centeredness, and outbursts of anger

....

Scorpio North Node, Taurus South Node

Develop: self-discipline, an interest in change and transformation, elimination of useless possessions, deep relationships, deep emotions, and sensuality

Leave behind: Overattachment to comfort, possessiveness, concern with ownership, stubbornness, and an obsession with sensual pleasures

....

Sagittarius North Node, Gemini South Node

Develop: a reliance on intuition, honesty, direct communication without censorship, search for truth, and a trust of self

Leave behind: second-guessing, indecisiveness, always wanting more information, saying what others want to hear, gossiping, and superficiality

....

Capricorn North Node, Cancer South Node

Develop: self-discipline, integrity, loyalty, the ability to stay goal-oriented, basing actions on reason rather than emotions, honoring successes, and self-responsibility

Leave behind: dependency, moodiness, insecurity leading to inaction, limiting self through fear, avoidance of personal risk, and control of others through emotional overplay

....

Aquarius North Node, Leo South Node

Develop: objectivity, intuitive knowing, wisdom, social idealism, a willingness to be unconventional, and group participation

Leave behind: an insistence on getting your own way, willfulness, attachment to the need for approval or a need to be the center of attention, and melodramatic tendencies

....

Pisces North Node, Virgo South Node

Develop: a nonjudgmental approach, compassion, a greater focus on the spiritual path, connection to higher states of consciousness, and expanded creativity

Leave behind: anxious reactions, overanalysis, a need for details and cleanliness, perfectionism, inflexibility, and faultfinding

The Saros Cycle

The moon is affected not only by the Earth's gravitational field but also by the powerful force of the sun, which causes it to "wobble" as it passes around the Earth. Therefore even though the moon takes twenty-eight to twenty-nine days to make one orbit of the Earth, it does not return to the exact same place in the sky until 18.6 years—nineteen eclipse years—have passed. This cycle was considered extremely important in Celtic and Mayan mythology because it acknowledged the creative relationship between the Earth, moon, and sun.

This sacred partnership is acknowledged in the town of Kildare in Ireland, were there is a perpetual fire dedicated to the virginal goddess of the hearth, Brigid or Brigit. In ancient times, this fire was located within the grounds of the cathedral and was watched over continuously by nineteen priestesses representing the nineteen-year cycle of the Celtic great year, or the Saros cycle. Each priestess took her turn to stay by the fire, knowing that on the twentieth day the fire would be tended by Brigid herself.

As we have learned, the true meaning of the archetype of the Virgin is to be complete unto yourself without the need for another to make you whole. Numerologically the number 19 is perfectly linked to this profound description of the Virgin. The number 1 represents beginnings and 9 represents completion. Together they add up to 10, the 0 of which represents the void where this perfect state is found.

Brigid's followers believe the physical fire absorbs the exquisite energy generated during the intimate dance between the sun, moon, and Mother Earth, transforming it into a continual source of joy, strength, and abundance that is available to everybody on this planet.

The ancient fire to Brigid was extinguished during the sixteenth century but was relit in 1993 and has remained alight since then. As we will later see, a similar fire was attended by the vestal virgins of Rome until it too was extinguished by those who did not understand the importance of the perpetual fire—and we all know what happened to the Roman Empire!

According to the Saros cycle, eclipses occur within the same sign of the zodiac every 18.6 years but not at the same geographical location. In fact, they appear 120 degrees farther around the globe. It is only after just under fifty-six years (3 × 18.6) that a triple Saros occurs—when the eclipse is seen both in the same sign and in the same location.

It's exciting to look at your life and ask yourself what important events occurred around the ages of 18.6, 37.2, 55.8, and then 74.5 years, as all these times are known as north and south node returns. As mentioned previously, these years will highlight what you are leaving behind and what you are developing. For women in particular, the third nodal return marks the end of our mothering years and the start of our crone years—at around fifty-six years old—when our focus of caring and creativity is less on the immediate family and more on creating a world worthy of the next seven generations.

When I look at my own life, I see that it was when I was eighteen that my father died, forcing me to listen to my Capricorn north node and become more self-reliant and disciplined while releasing my attachment to a very comfortable childhood. At thirty-eight, I was once again thrust out on my own after the breakdown of my first marriage, while, at the same time, my first book was published and I started to carve out a new path in my professional life. At fifty-six my life changed again as I chose to invest more energy in teaching and less in maintaining a full-time holistic health practice. I look forward in wonder to what my seventy-fourth year will bring!

The Saros Cycle Embedded in Ancient Sacred Sites

It is amazing to see that the builders of ancient sacred sites knew about this lunar cycle. When the first phase of Stonehenge was erected during the latter part of the fourth millennium BCE, the builders dug fifty-six holes just inside the outer earth bank (representing the years of a triple Saros cycle) that originally housed moveable wooden posts. Today the posts are no longer present, although white disks cover the holes. They're named Aubrey holes, after John Aubrey who discovered them in the seventeenth century.

The posts are thought to have been used to calculate lunar eclipses, reinforcing the suggestion that these ancient architects believed that such an event was not merely a spectacle but energetically caused a change in the subtle energies of the Earth and the consciousness of its people. Scientists are only now finding ways to measure these so-called subtle energies and are finding that, in fact, there is nothing subtle about their effects.

MOON STANDSTILLS

Another feature seen as significant to our ancestors is that there are times when the moon appears to be at a standstill, an event that occurs when the moon is approximately at right angles to its nodes.

During the winter months, the full moon appears ever higher in the sky until it reaches its maximum height above the visible horizon. This is the full moon closest to the winter solstice. In contrast, during the summer months the full moon appears ever lower in the sky until it reaches its lowest position. This is the full moon closest to the summer solstice. This movement is opposite that of the sun. The sun reaches its highest point above the horizon at the summer solstice and its lowest point at the winter solstice.

Due to the Saros cycle, however, every 18.6 years the moon reaches a maximum and minimum point above the horizon. These points were perceived by ancient peoples as being high and low points of fertility for both the land and its people. The next major lunar standstill will occur in 2025. The ancient people recorded both lunar and solar standstills in their sacred sites. These sites include Stonehenge, the Callanish Stones on the Isle of Lewis on the west coast of Scotland, and Chaco Canyon in New Mexico.

THE PRECESSION OF THE EQUINOXES

Without televisions and computers, our ancestors had plenty of time to study the celestial background in relation to the motions of planet Earth. But we now know some of these movements take thousands of years. Yet archaeological research shows clearly that ancient architects knew about the unique relationship between the Earth and the stars that make up the astrological constellations.

It may surprise you to know that such astrological knowledge is present in the most widely read book on the planet: the Bible. Deep within its pages we find mention of an astronomical and astrological process that reveals insights into the collective consciousness of our ancestors far beyond the reach of most historical texts.

These teachings relate to a process called *the precession of the equinoxes,* which describes a slow "wobble" of the Earth on its axis. One circle of this wobble takes approximately twenty-six thousand years, moving in the direction opposite to the normal rotation of the Earth. In other words, it appears to go backward through the astrological signs. It is because of this wobble that, if you were to point a camera at the North Star, Polaris, it would appear that all the other stars were orbiting around it, as in figure 8.2. However, over time, due to the wobble, the astronomical name of the North Star will change as the axis of the Earth points to a different star in the sky.

Figure 8.2. Movement of stars around the North Star

Astrologically, this means that approximately every two thousand one hundred and fifty years, the alignment of the Earth to the celestial equator changes, heralding in a new age or epoch and, with it, a new frequency of consciousness for humanity. The fact that there are references to these different epochs in the Bible clearly indicates that its authors understood the nature of the precession of the equinoxes, even though the concept is relatively unknown to today's scientists and scholars.

At present, with the transition from the age of Pisces to the Age of Aquarius, we are feeling the influence of both archetypal energies. The former—Pisces—is causing a large proportion of the population to give away their power to a higher authority, while the latter—Aquarius—reminds us that we *are* the authority.

The Age of Pisces the Fish
....
0 CE–2150 CE

Over the past two thousand years, under the influence of the fish, we have seen an expansion in religious and spiritual matters, mysticism, and creative endeavors. Just as one fish leads a shoal of fish, the age of Pisces has naturally spawned the appearance of many gurus and leaders who quickly attracted followers. These supporters are often only too happy to offer their leader their power in exchange for spiritual and material riches and the ability to avoid self-responsibility. This has led to the current state of affairs when far too much power and authority is being given to political, religious, medical, legal, and corporate leaders who can then be blamed when things go wrong. It's time to be self-accountable.

As we established earlier, the sign of Pisces is represented by two fish swimming in opposite directions united by a common band. The metaphysical meaning is best described as a sacred marriage of opposites or unity through the acceptance of diversity, mirroring the messages given by one of the messiahs of this Piscean age, Jesus (or Yeshua), who said: "Love thy neighbor as thy self" and "Do unto others as you would do unto yourself."

This seems like such simple advice to follow, especially for Christians. Indeed, they are wonderful messages for all of us, especially in this era that has the potential to see the unification of humanity. Yet this has probably been the bloodiest two millennia in the history of humanity. According to archaeologists, we've been more barbarous toward each other in these years than the previous five thousand years. Have we loved each other whatever anyone's creed, color, sexual orientation, or religion? No. We have gone to war against anybody who is not like us, especially the followers of different factions who see their way as the only way, a dogma underpinning battles even today.

To make matters worse, due to the Piscean tendency for addiction and delusion, we even go to war against our own disowned projections, without taking the responsibility to accept what we are doing.

Because this age birthed Christianity, many Christian principles are based on the archetypal energies of Pisces. The fish—the vesical piscis— is a common representation of the Christian faith, expressing unity or Christ consciousness. Interestingly, Jesus chose his disciples from fishermen, promised to "make them fishers of men," and involved water or fish in many of his miracles—such as walking on water, turning water into wine, and the feeding of five thousand with five loaves and two fish.

Our incessant tendency to express intolerance toward others or allow ourselves to be polarized into "us or them," whether politically, culturally, or even in sports, is destroying us as a species. Let us hope that, as this age draws to a close, we'll be able to see through the delusions, acknowledge our projections, and truly create a world based on oneness through the appreciation of diversity. If we don't change our ways, I'm not sure if we'll make it to the Age of Aquarius.

The Age of Aries the Ram
2150 BCE–0 CE

Aries is a masculine sign representing the warring and innovative ram. This epoch was a time for adventure, heroes, and the conquering of lands through physical strength. Hence there are stories of one army sending their bravest soldier to fight the hero of the other side at daybreak, with winner taking all. It is interesting to note that prior to around 1500 BCE, archaeologists have found very little evidence of mass weaponry and even war, reminding us that the desire to go to war to sort out our problems is not inevitable.

This age also speaks of courageously striking out to find new lands, as seen in the journey of the Israelites out of Egypt, led by none other than a guardian of rams: Moses the shepherd. He initially felt unworthy to be their leader until God told him to pick up a writhing snake from the ground and it became his staff or golden Djed of power.

Yet the people had not finished with the old epoch ruled by Hathor, the horned cow of Taurus, creating a golden calf when Moses's back was turned. His decision to give his people the drink of alchemically created gold probably forced them to finally leave behind the age of Taurus and embody the age of Aries.

It's fascinating to note that it was to the shepherds that the angel appeared to tell of the arrival of the messiah. And it was the shepherds—watchers over the sheep—who first offered gifts to the infant Jesus, handing over humankind's consciousness from the age of the ram to that of the fish.

The Age of Taurus the Cow

4300 BCE–2150 BCE

During the era of this female horned cow (not bull) there was an increase in matriarchal and agricultural societies, as the people relinquished their nomadic lifestyle, previously linked to the age of Gemini. At this point they began their co-cooperative relationship with the land. Hathor, the heavenly cow goddess, reigned supreme in Egypt, promising abundance to her people. Today many cultures still consider the cow to be sacred as a result of it having been so highly valued during this age.

It was during this time that both Judaism and Islam were conceived through the father Abraham. Yet the disharmony that still exists between these two great religions can be traced back to the discord between two mothers, Sarah and Hagar.

Until the time of Abraham, women lived in close communities, sharing husbands and the upbringing of children. But a great shift took place during Abraham's life, resulting in women losing their wealth and positions of power and becoming possessions of their men. This caused women to distrust each other, and they learned to fight to become the favorite wife in the hope this would assure the survival of their children.

So initially, the childless Sarah was perfectly happy for her husband, Abraham, to sleep with her handmaiden Hagar to produce an heir. But when Ismael was born and Sarah surprisingly gave birth to Isaac, Sarah became jealous and demanded that Hagar and Ismael be cast out into the desert. Yet God stepped in and promised both boys a different prosperous future, which led to the formation of the two religions but also the disharmony that has been the cause of so many wars over the years.

But the agrimony did not begin with Abraham or the boys. It arose from competitive discourse between two women at a crucial time in our history, the echoes of which are very present in many areas of society today, including within the corporate world.

Peace will come when women learn to forgive, trust, and support each other—for that is truly where our future lies.

The Age of Gemini the Twins
6450 BCE–4300 BCE

Little is known about this age, although it can be assumed, through our knowledge of astrological symbolism, that during these years the consciousness of the people was focused on the intellect and the development of increasingly advanced communication skills. Nomadic existence would also have been the order of the day, with a cross-pollination of ideas, philosophies, and language across the globe.

The Age of Cancer the Crab
8600 BCE–6450 BCE

As with the previous age, there are few signs remaining to inform us of the consciousness of the people during these years. Yet it's clear that the principles of the feminine would have taken precedence, thus making home, family, and nurturing major priorities. Since Cancer is a water sign, I wonder if this would have been a time of a great flood, when the people had to leave their Motherland and seek new pastures.

The Age of Leo the Lion
10,750 BCE–8600 BCE

During this age, personal power and authority were paramount. Humanity vied for supremacy, to be "king of the jungle." Yet that pride, plus the belief that humankind could control the elements and hence be more powerful than God or the Great Mother, also caused the downfall of the continent of Atlantis, which drowned under the emotional waters of its people's desires during this era.

Maybe the presence of the Sphinx in the Egyptian desert is there as a constant reminder of who is really in control. It is said that the half-human, half-lion figure symbolizes Sekhmet, the great crone lion goddess who is known to destroy anything that we try to possess for longer than its sell-by date! The Sphinx, known to be much older than the pyramids and made from natural rock, is scarred by the presence of salt water. This tells us that it was already carved when the area was last surrounded by seawater some nine to ten thousand years ago. This is estimated to be the period when the era of Atlantis finally came to an end by being submerged in waters that eventually became the Atlantic Ocean.

Figure 8.3. The famous and enigmatic Sphinx
Photo of the great Sphinx of Giza by MusikAnimal,
under Wikimedia Commons license CC BY-SA 3.0

The Age of Aquarius the Water Carrier
2150 CE–4300 CE

Today, as we are poised to enter the age of Aquarius, the zodiac sign that sits directly opposite Leo, I wonder what our ancient ancestors would say of our progress. In the Aquarian age it will no longer be possible to give your power away to another person and then blame them when things go wrong, for, unlike the Piscean age, everybody will be asked to be self-conscious and self-accountable. Rather than living in hierarchal societies where policies are made at the level of the central or federal government, power will return to communities who will make decisions that are best for everybody in the area.

At the same time, we will see everybody's contribution as equally important and unique, just as each piece is required to be in place to complete the jigsaw puzzle. There will be no need for leaders and messiahs, for everybody will be their own guru. Such a shift from giving power away to an authority figure to taking full responsibility for our thoughts, words, and actions will not be easy. We have become comfortable looking outside ourselves for solutions, encouraged by those who subversively perpetuate the pattern in order to continue to amass power. Yet times are changing, and despite the inconvenience of having to take responsibility for our creations, we will feel tremendous relief when we no longer have to:

- Spin plates to keep everybody happy
- Wear masks to avoid being seen fully or upsetting others
- Stay small so others aren't threatened by us
- Be the proverbial round peg in the square hole
- Carry ancestral baggage, fearful that if we lay it down, there will be no purpose to our life
- Continue to do something that, although we do it well, no longer makes our heart sing
- Convince ourselves that tomorrow will suffice when it comes to following our bliss

A clue of the times ahead was left by Jesus who, when asked by his disciples how they should find him, replied: "Behold, when you have entered the city, a man carrying a jar of water will meet you. Follow him into the house that he enters" (Luke 22:10). This water carrier is the symbol for the Age of Aquarius and reveals that the unified field of Christ consciousness will be found not in a single man but in everything and everybody on this planet. Our greatest challenge now is to stop playing mindless games of judging everybody who is different and find ways of truly "loving thy neighbor as thy self," which begins with loving ourselves.

9

MYTHOLOGICAL ARCHAEOLOGY

Heaven onto Earth

As today's archaeologists dig ever deeper into our past, they are often left bemused and amazed by the architectural and engineering feats of our ancestors, which, even with modern technology, may still be irreproducible. There is a tendency to see every sacred site that aligns to a solstice or equinox as a mere calendar to guide farmers when to plant or harvest their crops. In truth, these sites were built to connect the ever-changing inspirational design of heaven with the creative power of the earth. The ancient architects' ability to create a simple window or passageway within a stone structure to align with a cosmic event millions of miles away is astonishing.

Clearly the ancient people had a far greater understanding about our relationships, not only with Mother Earth, but with the cosmic forces. They believed that our purpose on this planet is to manifest the beauty and magnificence of the Great Mother's abundance here on Earth. Their megalithic buildings, sacred temples, and passage wombs, still standing after more than four thousand years, are a testament to their brilliance.

Let's explore some of these sacred sites now.

SPECIFIC ASTRONOMICAL
AND ARCHITECTURAL FEATURES
OF THE WORLD'S SACRED SITES

To understand the Great Mother's plan to create heaven on Earth and how cosmic events and planetary movements affect not only the evolution of human consciousness but also that of the Earth, it's valuable to look at some of the special design characteristics that accompanied the building of many of the sacred sites around the world, including those found in Britain, Ireland, Central and South America, Egypt, and throughout Europe.

Different sites have different purposes but all are connected to the creative cycles of life. Some sacred sites are natural, such as mountains, geothermal springs, a fairy fort of trees, or a cenote, which is a natural sinkhole formed from the collapse of limestone bedrock that exposes spring water underneath.

The earliest sacred sites were not built merely for human burial or spiritual transformation. Indeed, it is probable that an etheric temple was in place long before humans took physical form and may have been used by star people or interdimensional beings especially in the early days of planet Earth. Some sacred temples were formed in the higher dimensions of the holographic field, unseen and "undiscovered" until our consciousness reached a vibration high enough to draw them down into the third dimension. That is why places like the temple complex of Machu Picchu lay relatively unnoticed until 1911. Even though the original buildings were erected in the fifteenth century, it is clear that these mountains have acted as energetic hotspots for thousands of years.

Temples were built to act as an intermediary vessel between heaven and Gaia, our living, breathing Mother Earth; to be the womb of new creation or the tomb of old consciousness whose time to die had arrived. Most stone-based ancient temples are built so that their entry points align to different phases of the moon or sun—especially to sunrises, sunsets, equinoxes, and solstices. There are also temples that align to the apparent movement of the Pleiades constellation or the planet Venus.

Figure 9.1. Machu Picchu

Others are planned to be oriented to a much slower movement—the precession of the equinoxes. Each celestial body is believed to carry a specific archetypal energy or frequency, so that when a particular planet or star is highlighted, the particular inspirational fire of that planet will enter the Earth. For instance, the Maya kept a watchful eye on the movement of the planet Venus, for when she appeared as the morning star it was time to plant crops or go to war but when she was the evening star, it was time to be reflective and rest.

Running beneath our feet is a feminine serpentine grid guarded by dragon energy. This grid carries the Great Mother's primordial energy of creation. It was laid down into the structure of Mother Earth at the beginning of life on this planet. Also known as *spirit lines, song lines,* or *fairy lines,* the grid contains the matrix or blueprint for everything that will ever be created on our planet. This grid, containing the potential for all conscious creation, is just waiting for us to look downward not skyward to access our brilliance and abundance.

An analogy to understand this union of heaven and earth would be to imagine an acorn falling to the ground. Immediately it sends roots into the earth's serpentine grid to connect with the already present energetic blueprint of an oak tree. After a while, we see the new shoots of a young oak tree pushing up through the soil, stretching toward the light of the sun. But the power to grow comes from the continual nurturing provided by the feminine energetic grid within Mother Earth. This is very similar to our own spiritual growth.

Many may have heard of ley lines that exist at the level of the etheric body of the planet and move in a wavy manner. Our ancestors built churches and temples where the ley lines meet. The serpentine grid is much deeper than ley lines. Its energy runs across the planet in a more haphazard manner, being drawn to any structures that are round—such as mountains, wells, lakes, or caves—where it can curl inside. This causes such places to be seen as highly potent with consciousness waiting to be fertilized. When lightning strikes a mountain, or the sun's rays hit the water in a well, that particular consciousness is released into the world, first affecting the people living nearby.

Even though our star, the sun, is often seen as just a ball of fire, metaphysically it is much more. Our sun is an interdimensional portal or doorway into multidimensional worlds and ultimately to the Central Sun of the Central Sun, or the source of the fire of inspiration. This is why each morning at sunrise, it is good to stand on Mother Earth and tap into the blueprint of your soul's destiny, located in the heart chakra. Then, moving your awareness to the soles of your feet, send roots into the serpentine grid and then draw up into your body creative dreams from the ocean of possibilities. Try not to think about what you want to embody, allowing your heart to choose what is right for the day. When the energy reaches the third eye, close your eyes and let the first light of the sun enter the third eye, fertilizing your dreams to life. It is then that we may find ourselves saying, "Ah-ha, I know what I'm going to do today!"

A similar birthing experience bringing new consciousness to the planet is witnessed in sites aligned to the winter solstice, such as

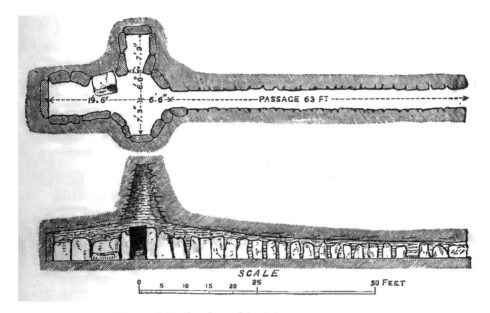

Figure 9.2. Sketches of the Newgrange passage
Sketches by William Frederick Wakeman from
the 1903 edition of *Wakeman's Handbook of Irish Antiquities*

Newgrange. As the new sun's rays, carrying the seeds of inspiration, pass into the passageway of the temple, they enter the serpentine grid, fertilizing the blueprint to form life, just as the sperm fertilizes an egg—focus to create meets force to create.

After three days, the energy of this newly fertilized conscious-ness is shared throughout the world via streams of water, the roots of the trees, and the serpentine grid itself. The chambers at the end of Newgrange's birth canal mirror the unique sacred geometry of a woman's regenerative and nurturing organs. Both the vesica piscis, symbol of love, and the golden mean, symbol of spiraling creativity, are present.

All sacred sites, whether man-made such as Stonehenge or natural such as Uluru, are calling on us now to open our hearts, root ourselves into Mother Earth, and receive the new seeds of consciousness that are arriving on these amazing celestial waves. It is time to create heaven on Earth.

Figure 9.3. Stonehenge

Figure 9.4. Uluru

CELESTIAL COMMUNICATION

There is one more type of building that was designed to enhance communication and flow of energy between heaven and earth. Built during the time of the Sumerian moon god Nanna, towers or observatories called *ziggurats* were designed both as places to study celestial movements and to worship the moon from the temple that sat atop the structure. The Babylonians continued the tradition of lunar worship under the guidance of their moon god Sin. Could the followers of the pagan moon god Sin be behind the word *sinful*?

It would be wrong to assume these were unsophisticated people baying at the moon. On the contrary, records show the Babylonians were a highly developed civilization with a deep understanding of the sciences—including medicine, chemistry, alchemy, botany, zoology, mathematics, and astronomy.

The most famous of the Babylonian ziggurats was known as the Tower of Babel, constructed in what is now southern Iraq. The mathematical precision incorporated into the design suggests a desire to synthesize their profound understanding of universal energies with experiences within the unified field of nonlocal reality—in other words, to know the immortality of the gods.

From the Bible, we learn about the demise of this tower due to the fact that the God of the day is concerned when he sees the people have built a tower with its top in the heavens so they may remain together as one unit.

> The Lord said, "Behold, they are one people, and they have all one language, and this is only the beginning of what they will do. And nothing that they propose to do will now be impossible for them. Come, let us go down and there confuse their language, so that they may not understand one another's speech." So the Lord dispersed them from there over the face of all the earth, and they left off building the city.

Figure 9.5. The Tower of Babel
"The Tower of Babel" or "Turris Babel"
from Anthanasius Kircher, Amsterdam, 1679

From this story comes the origin of the verb to *babble,* interpreted as "to speak incoherently so others cannot understand you." We could interpret this text to mean that God saw that, in having one voice, humankind could challenge his will. But other interpretations suggest that God stepped in "for our own good," as he believed we would self-destruct without his guidance. Thus he caused separation between the people, forming diverse nations in order to bring peace.

If this interpretation is correct, it's clear the plan didn't work! I suspect the greatest cause of humanity's destructive nature is the very fact we do not have a common language to unite us. This is not merely a matter of verbal expression. What's missing is our ability to *speak and hear* the common language of the Great Mother's heart: the language of love.

Perhaps as we enter the unified realm of ether we are once again being given the chance to reconnect to the language of oneness with the ability to "hear" each other's feelings, desires, and thoughts through the purity of our hearts.

SURFING THE WAVES OF CHANGE

One final note concerning our relationship with Mother Earth; it's clear that we are witnessing increasing numbers of natural disasters such as earthquakes, erupting volcanoes, floods, fires, and hurricanes all around the globe. This is not, as many want us to believe, because Mother Earth is angry with humanity; such emotions are human not planetary. It is more accurate to say that, like us, Gaia or Mother Earth is seeking to reach her own state of perfect unity and is shedding old patterns or structures that limit her growth.

Let's be clear: the planet does not need us to save her; we are not her guardians but her guests and presently very poor guests. In fact, we are more like fleas on her back that she could shake off in a moment. But if we truly wish to transform to our state of natural perfection along with Mother Earth, then the best way to surf the waves of change is by loving the piece of the planet each of us was given at birth to nurture—our own physical body. Love on it, live in it, and enjoy it; then Gaia will perhaps carry us together into the new world of ether.

PART THREE

The Twelve Stages of Evolution and Dissolution

In part 3, the concluding section of this book, we will embark on a voyage of self-discovery and enlightenment, recognizing that the twelve astrological steps we're about to encounter have been taken by mystics for thousands of years in their search for eternal life. Understandably, our starting point is the ocean of possibilities, where everything waits in suspended animation until we are inspired to turn our attention to one particular area of dynamic potentiality, stimulating a whole new cycle of creativity to begin with our next in-breath.

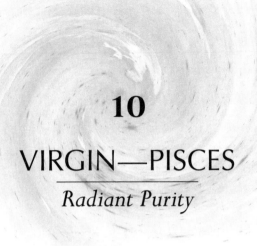

10

VIRGIN—PISCES
Radiant Purity

Pisces

Alchemy: coagulation; one with all consciousness
Polarity: feminine; the Virgin, soul, the unmanifested self that
  is complete within itself
Moon Phase: dark moon phase

Naturally we begin our journey in the primordial waters of the Great Mother, who waits with anticipation for us to throw our line into her ocean of possibilities and draw toward us the seeds of inspiration that will ignite our passion to create until we reach a successful conclusion. She does offer a couple of suggestions:

1. *Maybe it would be a good idea to choose a different length of fishing line than the one you usually use.*
2. *Perhaps you're ready to walk a little further along the shoreline so that you can cast your line into an area of water that is unknown to you, offering new, exciting, and mysterious possibilities.*

Then she steps back and watches with pride as we step forward to claim our destiny.

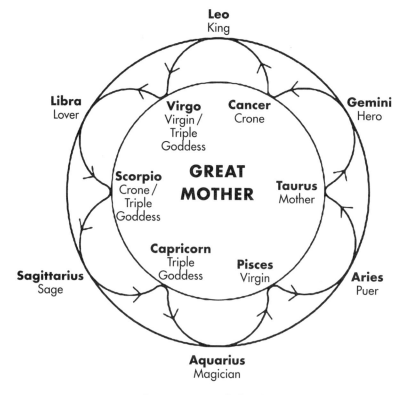

Figure 10.1. The creative cycle leading to eternal life
Image by Sherrie Frank

THE UNLIMITED IMAGINATION OF PISCES

The astrological sign linked with this dynamic state of potentiality is Pisces, symbolized by two fish swimming in opposite directions, joined at their center. Common characteristics that are found in someone who has strong Pisces energies in their astrological natal chart are that they have a highly developed imagination, a belief of being unlimited, strong intuition, the ability to manifest whatever they focus upon, and tendencies toward addiction, delusion, and madness! It is vitally important for such people to undergo regular reality checks and then they can truly create magic.

As discussed previously these two fish are held in dynamic tension by their joint energies, expressing both the dream to be created and the fully realized form—complete unto itself—the true meaning of the Virgin. In other words, if we are excited by an idea, then it has already manifested fully somewhere in the universe. If we fail to feel the excitement, then the dream was either never meant to see the light of day or somehow we have missed a turn and need to retrace our steps until we feel that same enthusiasm again.

At the same time, when we admire someone, we are seeing what may be just a vague idea in our mind already in fully created form right in front of our eyes. At this point, I hear some people say, "Well if they are living my dream, why should I bother? Why should I continue to try to make my dream a reality?" Because the reason we attract such a person into our life is not to discourage us but to cheer us on as we give our unique twist to the expression of this idea.

If the eyes are the window to the soul and it's impossible to see our own eyes except in a mirror, we attract people who show us the potential of who we are in our wholeness—whether we like what we see or not! The same dynamic is reflected in the yin and yang symbol (see figure 10.2) where the "eye" of each fish is the seed of the fully realized form of the other fish. Holding the two fish together in the sign of Pisces is a golden link symbolizing the fluidic central force that is the source of their existence and is fed by the flow of creative energy that is produced when two diverse forces interact. This symbiotic trinity is a theme that

Figure 10.2. The yin and yang symbol

repeats itself throughout our journey, reminding us that we need each other to become whole. We are social beings who all start life attached to someone.

HEARING THE CALL OF THE INTUITION

As we float in the ocean of possibilities we know we are home, held in the warm embrace of the Great Mother's heart. Like droplets of water that lose their individuality when they become part of a mighty ocean, we are no longer alone and are ecstatic. We are intimately connected to the All-Oneness of the Great Mother and are seen and known in our wholeness with nothing to hide.

You may ask, "Why would any of us want to leave this state of bliss to experience a life on Earth with all its struggles, suffering, and uncertainty?" The answer is simple: because we love the Great Mother.

Let us look at life on Earth from a multidimensional point of view. What if this planet is not a physical place but a hologram produced by the synthesis of different states of consciousness, especially emotions and beliefs—the energy and design behind creation? What if the planet is a playground of creative potential with powerful fire at its core providing us with the feminine force to create? What if our purpose on Earth is to bring into manifestation the unrealized potential that exists within the Great Mother's ocean of possibilities and eventually bring the seeds of wisdom back to the Great Mother so her consciousness can grow?

We have probably lived many lifetimes in this playground, happily using the tools and elements provided to assemble all manner of products, some of which we like and some of which we instantly reject.

But there is a deeper problem: many of us have forgotten our reason to create, the purpose for being on this beautiful blue planet. We have become overwhelmed by the emotions that are evoked during interactions between us and our own creations. Perversely, we have become addicted to these sticky feelings even if this means we attract more pain and suffering. In an attempt to break free, we have often created beliefs to make sense of the pain but instead of freeing us so we can reconnect to the heart of the Great Mother, such dogmas often just trap us in a world that is devoid of self-love, love of our fellow human beings, or the belief that we are loved by the Great Mother. Ultimately, in our anger and pain, we battle against or go to war against our own creations.

For in truth, everything we see around us is a holographic representation of our own heart and mind, created by us so that we may know ourselves and therefore once again experience the bliss of unity consciousness: unconditional love. To break free of our addictions, we first have to accept that we have a problem and recognize that perhaps all we think is real, even our religious and spiritual belief is just a construct of the mind. Remember the mind is filled with facts already experienced; only the heart can set us free.

As we release our hold on illusionary beliefs, our trust in the part of us that never leaves us—our soul—becomes stronger. It is our greatest friend because, as an aspect of the divine spark, we would not exist without it. Our soul, located in our heart chakra, speaks to us through the intuition or inner knowing of the Virgin.

For many years I have taught classes on intuition and found that most people, whether they know it or not, are intuitive to varying degrees. They receive insights from their soul through various sources such as dreams, precognition of future events, the messages of the body during illness, feeling the energy of others, or just by knowing what is right. But the sad part of the story is that many people do not follow through on these insights. They become distracted by apparently more important issues, decide that the idea of change will be too much of a burden on their family, or convince themselves that tomorrow is soon enough.

Ultimately, the real reason that we don't follow through on our intuition is that we are being asked to face the mystery of the unknown where the outcome is not predetermined. This is when it becomes clear that our mind is controlling our life rather than our heart.

Despite the clarity of our soul's call, the true purpose or outcome of following the intuition is often concealed as if to test our faith.

Indeed, the very fact that I live in the United States resulted from an innocent question that someone asked me soon after the death of my mother. I heard myself say with undeniable certainty, "I am going to live in America," and because I seemed so sure of myself, nobody questioned my decision. Responding to an intuitive insight might sound extremely reckless to those who would never leave home without adequate financial resources and a specific plan of action, and yet it is this mix of excitement and natural anxiety that often births our next best step.

So are you ready to:

- Be seen and heard for who you are?
- Hear the Virgin's intuitive calls, where each message resonates with the pulse of the soul and excites the dream into reality?
- Stop making excuses or finding clever distractions to ignore the call to action?
- Allow the sweet feelings of love from the Great Mother to persuade you to take that leap of faith?

Everybody has had the experience of following their intuition at some point in their life. When following this pulse of the soul, we often experience a sense of peace, strength, contentment, and joy. The decision to act on these insights feels so right, we don't even ask other people for their opinion: we just do it, just as I strongly knew I should leave Britain and go to America without knowing why.

At the same time, most of us have experiences when we went against the wisdom of our soul, choosing to follow the desires of our personality. When I asked a student "When did you know you shouldn't have married your husband of twenty-five years?" she answered "The day before the wedding." I'm sure we can all tell similar stories when we turned our back on our soul and perhaps lived to regret it or spent years convincing ourselves that being miserable is just part of our karma.

But the Virgin is very patient: she holds on to the blueprint of our incarnation, until we are ready to hear her still, small voice. She urges us on when we become paralyzed with fear, sits with us when we're weary and in need of rest, and celebrates with us when we resonate with the light of our true nature. She wants us to know that:

- There is no judgment of our actions except within our own minds
- If we do something well but are no longer growing from the situation, it's probably time to let go and enter the unknown realms of mystery
- True control comes from following the unpredictable but certain call of the soul
- The Great Mother loves us unconditionally whatever we do

I suggest keeping a journal to write down any intuitive insights or new ideas that pop into your mind.

Here are some more simple tips to help you follow your intuition:

1. Three times rule: if you hear about the same idea three times, do it!
2. Ask for help: the universe or spirit world is very keen that we should fulfill our destiny in this life. If there is a question, especially about whether you are on the right path, call on your spiritual guidance before you go to sleep and ask, "Close all the doors not in harmony with my soul and open those doors that are."
3. If you have questions about your participation in an event or within a relationship ask, "If I'm not supposed to do this thing or be with this person, make it very clear for me now." When tickets go missing or the car won't start, don't panic but rather thank the universe for its help.
4. If you know you have an active mind, meditation may not be the best way to receive intuitive insights. It is better to spend time each day in an activity that doesn't require much thought but will occupy the logical left brain, such as showering, gardening, cooking, or walking. This then allows the intuitive right brain to talk to you unimpeded.
5. In the same way, if you have a question and need to bypass your logical brain, you can find the answer by crafting a poem from your heart,

singing the response, or writing your question with your dominant hand and answering it with the nondominant hand.

6. Remember the spirit world cannot interfere with your free will, but it can throw opportunities and advice your way; it is essentially your choice whether you listen.

In essence, the Virgin never leaves us, we just have to make sure we don't close our hearts to her love.

11

BOY-CHILD—ARIES
The Child or Ego Is Born

Aries

Alchemy: calcination; stepping beyond the confines of the collective

Polarity: masculine; puer or boy-child, adventure, curiosity, and innocence

Moon Phase: new; to germinate and emerge

The next five phases of the spiritual journey (see figure 11.1) describe the growth and development of the dream or idea as it pushes its way from its resting place within the Earth, strengthens its core, and ultimately stands tall and proud, king of all it surveys. Together, the stages represent the development of the first length of the magician's wand, known esoterically as the *ida*, which runs along our spine from base chakra to crown.[1] During the journey, energy is transformed from the frequencies of spirit into the frequencies of matter as the boy-child becomes king.

At this critical time in our history, this half of the cycle is in some ways less important than the final stages that ask for the king to descend into the realm of the Crone and claim the gems of wisdom that he will eventually gift to the Great Mother. Yet our ability to fulfill our spiritual destiny is predetermined by the strength of our

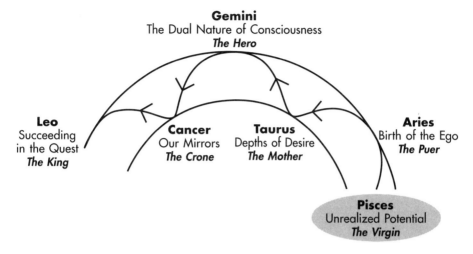

Figure 11.1. Five stages of inspiration

Image by Sherrie Frank

successes, for it is this energy that will sustain us during our passage through the underworld.

BIRTH OF THE EGO

During a lifetime we're reborn many times, on each occasion emerging from the Great Mother's ocean as a newborn child, eager to start again and perhaps do things differently based on the wisdom of past experiences. Under the protection of the Virgin, we are motivated to leave the safety and comfort of the known and seek our own unique individuality. This is also known as the birth of the ego.

It is the Virgin who drops the seed of an idea into the chalice of our mind, knowing that perhaps a certain amount of time will need to pass before the idea sees the light of day. It is the Virgin's intuitive voice that whispers in our ear at the moment of our waking, causing us to exclaim for no explicit reason: "Ah-ha! Today is the day!"

The sign of Aries—representing the Ram—is a masculine sign that often reminds me of a young adventurous boy who leaves the safety of his mother's home to explore his surroundings. He throws objects, climbs trees, and performs outrageous tricks, just because he can. He is not malevolent and there are consequences to his actions, but he typically picks himself up, learns from the experience, and moves on.

Generally, even though Aries is a fire sign and hence can become fired up and angry—especially when told he/she must wait—the flame of his/her anger is short lived, leaving a minimal post-fire imprint.

This passion for adventure without the heavy load of disappointment when things don't work out as we would like is essential for this stage of our journey. We see this same adventurous spirit in a child learning to walk. After a few steps, they land softly back onto the cushion of their diapers without shedding a tear. A few minutes later, off they go again. No toddler has ever said, "That's it; I'm not going to walk, it's too difficult!"

The impetus for the boy-child to begin a new project, take a risk, or seek new pastures comes from the fire within the base chakra— a passion for growth and adventure. It is from this place that we develop hobbies, activities chosen by us in search of joy and pleasure rather than from a sense of duty. But this sense of individual freedom to find joy in what we do, without external conditioning, may be challenged by the fact that this chakra is also linked to a need for security, which in turn is commonly associated with a need to belong to a tribe. Such tribal belonging can be found in family, gender, culture, religion, political group, or sports team, all possessing their own set of tight rules that need to be followed to avoid alienation and rejection by the tribe.

Our fear of abandonment often overrides our Aries-inspired spirit of adventure, keeping us focused on obeying strict, ingrained, and unspoken edicts that begin with words such as *should, must,* or *can't.* It is not uncommon to be completely unaware that we're following these dictates, so deeply are they embodied in our psyche and that of our ancestors. The ultimate fear of not "fitting in" is loneliness and yet, in truth, we can be lonely in a crowd. This is because in our attempt to conform to the rules, it is not unusual for us to lose ourselves. In truth, when we believe that we are in control of our life we may in fact be controlled by fear and not even recognize the brain washing. But don't worry, the Virgin is always present. She encourages our boy-child to remember that life is an adventure so we can start to take back control of our lives in small and simple ways, until we feel secure enough to act outside the range of tribal approval.

My suggestions for restoring the sense of adventure and enhancing security of the self:

1. Begin by taking fifteen minutes in the day to do something that is not focused on a goal or outcome but that brings you pleasure.
2. If you find that the "shoulds" and "musts" invade this quiet space, you know you have a problem. Turn the need for structure to your advantage by consciously dedicating time each day or week to activities that are not linked to someone else's schedule.
3. Remember to breathe out long and deeply into your feet on a regular basis to release all the chatter of your mind.
4. Lay aside special times for hobbies, personal activities that light your inner fire.

The base chakra was not always the source of belonging. Within many cultures, over three millennia ago, when a baby was born, their placenta was buried within Mother Earth and a tree planted on top of it. This signified the fact that although the physical mother provides comfort during the early months of life, her role is to eventually wean the child off the breast and root them in Mother Earth who is, in truth, their lifetime source of nourishment and security.

The reason behind this practice is to connect the child to their root chakra—located about nine feet or three meters beneath our feet—and hence to the Great Mother's grid of consciousness flowing through this energy center. Once the child taps into this grid they instantly know that they belong not only to their soul but, through this, to the heart of the Great Mother, a connection that cannot be broken. It was only with the rise of the patriarchy that our access to this grid and to the

Great Mother's love was cut off, reflected in mythological stories that described the killing of serpents and dragons.

Here is a meditation that helps to root us into Mother Earth's grid on a regular basis, bringing peace and stability while also stimulating us to step beyond limiting beliefs and walk our own path. This is a more profound practice than grounding, as it allows us to connect to our unique blueprint of perfection.

Make sure you are in a quiet and safe place where you are able to close your eyes; you may stand or sit for this meditation.

Take a few deep breaths to quiet your mind, breathing out right down to your feet. Then move your awareness to your heart chakra—center of your chest—and connect to the deep love of your soul. Then with your feet on the ground become aware of magnets on the soles of your feet and that there is an even larger magnet in Mother Earth. Surrendering to her love, allow yourself to sink into the Earth, developing roots from the soles of your feet that go in all directions. Allow the moist and loving soil of Mother Earth to surround and nurture your roots without suffocation. Nest into her love. When you are ready, send your awareness to the end of one of your deepest roots—the root chakra. Through this runs the golden serpentine energy of consciousness carrying all your dreams and ideas. Gently draw this energy up along your roots and legs and into the base chakra, stimulating that Aries sense of adventure. Let the energy containing your ideas move up to the heart chakra where it resonates with your soul's blueprint, bringing the dream alive. Finally, you can allow the golden energy to move up and out of the crown chakra like a fountain, creating a golden bubble of invigorating energy full of the promise of creative activity.

So now are you ready to reclaim:

◉ Your right to a true sense of belonging, releasing your need to abide by the limiting man-made rules of tribal energy?
◉ The dreams and ideas given to you by the Virgin but that have been gathering dust in closets, because they did not fit in with the ideals and plans of the tribe?

Let's evoke that Aries sense of adventure, plant our unique seeds, and see them grow, remembering that because we are distinct beings, other people may not always understand our process or be unable to offer encouragement. But that is okay, as we are surrounded by love and we can always ask our spiritual guides to keep us on the right path by saying, "If this dream is not meant to see the light of day, please make that very clear now." When the seedling doesn't grow, remember that our soul may just want us to step onto the path, before it leads us off in another direction.

You see, our inner guidance knows the type of "candy" or "carrot" required to induce us onto the path, certain that once our commitment is guaranteed, any change in the agenda is unlikely to throw us off course and we will gladly move forward. You may in fact remember a time when the stranger sitting next to you at a seminar became more influential to your soul's destiny than the speaker you had paid to hear. Or you may remember that you followed the love of your life to another state or country, only to fall out of love with the person and in love with the location. In other words, it is not always important that our boy-child knows why or where we're traveling. All we have to do is agree to the adventure.

As this chapter comes to an end, please ask yourself:

- ◉ What ideas or activities excite me, filling my heart with joy?
- ◉ What would I regret never having taken the risk to begin?
- ◉ How would my life change if my life wasn't driven by *should, must,* or *ought to?*
- ◉ What recent inspirational ideas have I received from the Virgin that are still waiting for me to take the first step toward manifestation?
- ◉ If I knew I couldn't fail and would always be loved whatever I did, what would I do differently?

As a woman once asked me in a lecture: "Jesus came to me five years ago in a meditation, gave me a paintbrush, and said I should paint: What should I do?" If the masters take the time to visit, please do not wait another twenty-six thousand years to manifest your destiny!

12

MOTHER—TAURUS

Diving into the Depths of Desire

Taurus

Alchemy: dissolution; discovering the gifts and talents that lie within

Polarity: feminine; Mother, nurturing, possessions, skills, and talents

Moon Phase: crescent; to move forward through focused attention

In order to fulfill his ideas and dreams, the boy-child must focus his attention on the abundance offered by the Great Mother and draw toward him all those things that will nurture him on his journey. This phase, under the watchful guidance of the matriarchal energy of Taurus the cow, reveals to us our inner wealth of skills, talents, and gifts that ultimately will underpin our success as king.

TAURUS THE COW

As a sign, Taurus is generous, practical, very talented, creative, and loves all things sensual—including taste, touch, smell, texture, music, and food! These traits are very evident when someone has strong Taurean qualities in their natal astrology chart. Yet these individuals can also be stubborn with a tendency to underplay their gifts and talents even to the extent of shooting themselves in the foot rather than sharing their gifts with others. This quirk in their nature is linked to a deep-seated fear of losing their most prized possessions in the belief that they offer security, including their gifts. They would rather bury their talents than share them with the world.

So when facing this stage of the journey, we need to be mindful that when we have the courage to share our skills and gifts, our seeds will receive the nurturing they need. Sometimes, however, it is not always easy to appreciate our unique gifts and talents because when something comes easily to us, we may take it for granted. At other times, our gifts and talents may not have been celebrated by family, teachers, or even friends; possibly due to their own feelings of inadequacy. It is also very hard when a child's skills are compared with those of their siblings or even of their parents, making their unique talents less than important.

I suggest you make a list of your top six talents. These are usually skills that you both enjoy and excel in. If you write, "I'm good at caring for others," what makes your caring unique? Is it that you are thoughtful, are a good listener, enjoy making others feel comfortable, or can intuitively meet others' needs? If you list creativity as a skill, how does that appear in the world: through watercolor painting, quilt work, cooking, or gardening? And is your creativity spontaneous or do you like to follow a pattern?

I've met people who have been told they are going to be a writer or healer by a spiritual medium only to reply, when asked if they enjoy writing or like people, "Not at all!" If you find writing boring, then this is a clear indication that writing is probably not one of your talents. Sometimes however, a special gift may have been present in childhood and then lost when life took a dramatic turn toward survival, poverty, or responsibility. Reclaiming it from the depths of the box of childhood memories is a wonderful feeling.

Now it's time to apply these nurturing juices to your precious seed, just as a gardener would not just toss a plant into the earth in the hope that it will root itself and survive. As a gardener myself, I know we prepare the soil, add nutrients, dig an adequately deep hole, and water the plant regularly. So the next questions to ask are:

- ◉ What period of time am I going allocate to the nurturing of my dreams? Mark it in your calendar.

- ◉ Which of my talents are particularly important to the growth of this seed?

- ◉ Are there ideas that I received but then forgot to water? It's never too late to go back and restart the process.

- ◉ Do I need to enlist the help of others to ensure my dream continues to grow? Never ask someone who has never experienced success themselves.

- ◉ How will I know when my gifts are ready to share with the world and that I am only holding on to them through fear? Perhaps sharing your progress in a blog or asking your friends to encourage you will keep you moving in the right direction.

MEETING OUR MENTOR

During this phase it's not uncommon to encounter people who offer wisdom and guidance for the journey ahead. Exhibiting the Mother energy, this character is known as a mentor and in mythological tales was traditionally dressed as an old man or woman, symbolic of the archetype of the sage, mystic, or hermit. Such archetypes usually appear to be "in the world but not of it" and hence may accompany the traveler for a while before disappearing or dying. Thus we meet Merlin in the Arthurian legends, Gandalf in *Lord of the Rings,* Obi-Wan Kenobi and Master Yoda in *Star Wars,* and the fairy godmother in the *Cinderella* tale.

In fictional stories, mentors often possess a magical and mysterious quality, leaving us with little doubt that their supernatural qualities are a result of their own internal battles and the eventual mastery of their darker energies. Such strength reminds us that those who step up as mentors must be selflessly dedicated to the task, unattached to any specific outcome, and not seeking self-gratification.

◉ Thinking back, especially into your childhood or teenage years, can you name three people who acted as your mentors by offering support, encouragement, and nurturing of your dreams? Maybe they were a member of your family, a teacher, a neighbor, or someone who "saw you" when you were still floundering in the shadows. As mentioned above, they often walk with us for a short while before leaving.

◉ Which of your qualities or skills did your mentors evoke during your time with them?

I remember a friend mentioning an elderly neighbor who would invite her into the home to see this woman's fine collection of books, carefully kept in a library that smelled of ageless wisdom. My friend told me that she was in awe of this collection, as there were few books in her childhood home to read. Over the years, this old lady taught her mentee not only to read but sparked her curiosity to learn, the joy of adventure, and the desire to pass this knowledge on to others. My friend became a high school teacher.

I've been privileged to meet a number of special spiritual mentors in my life. Some walked with me for mere minutes and others supported my journey for years. Not all were comfortable to be around, and yet there was no doubt they loved me, and I certainly wouldn't be where I am now without them. Three of the most significant mentors were men, each dying suddenly, seventeen years apart. The first was my loving and adventurous father, who protected and supported my physical and human nature until I was ready and able to take care of myself. Seventeen years later, I met a great love who opened my heart to my emotional and transpersonal self; he died tragically soon after our meeting. Finally, I was privileged to meet a wonderful kahuna, or wise man from Hawaii, who joyously supported my spiritual being for three years before being killed in a car accident. His contribution to my soul completed the mentoring of my body, heart, and spirit. I feel blessed to have been acknowledged, encouraged, and loved by these three amazing men, all of whom still watch over me from beyond the veil.

13

HERO—GEMINI

The Dual Nature of Consciousness

Gemini

Alchemy: separation; owning one's own power to make decisions

Polarity: masculine; hero, strength, and resourcefulness

Moon Phase: first quarter; to build and decide

Every culture has its heroes, their grand accomplishments displayed for all to see, in the hope this will encourage others to follow in their wake.

- ◉ Who would you consider a hero in your life?
- ◉ If you can think of more than one, is there a common theme that runs through all those you consider heroes?
- ◉ What qualities do you think a hero should possess?
- ◉ Do you identify with your heroes?

All heroes have one thing in common: they are destined to make a journey that is both physical and spiritual in the quest for personal fulfillment. The greatest study of heroes was carried out by the late Joseph Campbell, whose book *The Hero with a Thousand Faces* has sold millions of copies around the world.[1] Within his teachings he reminds us that despite the tendency to place idolized individuals on a pedestal, the hero exists within everyone. This is the part of us that steps courageously into the unknown, enjoys adventure, overcomes obstacles, and strives toward contentment, whether the focus is on our inner or outer life.

OWNING OUR TWIN POWERS

To become a hero we first need to extract two unique strengths from the Great Mother: our physical and spiritual powers. They are to be found within the astrological sign of Gemini, which speaks of the male twins Castor and Pollux who, since one was immortal and the other mortal, could rarely be together. They therefore made a decision to both constantly move between heaven and earth, meeting in the middle for a few exquisite moments of delight.

This restlessness and a tendency toward boredom are noticeable features in anyone with Gemini dominant in their astrological natal chart. A desire to talk, teach, and write is also usually present, reflecting their ability—through their journeys between heaven and earth—to be messengers of information especially of a spiritual nature. The downside of this constant movement is a tendency to be described as "two-faced," one minute fascinated by a conversation and then off to find more interesting pastures, like a bee that goes from flower to flower to collect the juicy nectar.

Castor and Pollux represent the twin forces of spiritual-feminine and physical-masculine strength that transform the boy into a hero as he learns to master these essential forces of creation.

Each of these twin powers is only as strong as the relationship it has with the other; the natural tension between them leads to reciprocally rewarding growth. This is the same dynamic that exists between the two fish of the astrological sign of Pisces. Their natural friction supports and is supported by the link connecting them.

As long as the hero maintains a healthy respect for both his spiritual-intuitive and physical-intellectual natures, then both will serve him well, nurturing his eternal being. Should either take priority, however, or should the flow between them become blocked or broken, our hero's journey will become limited both in terms of material success and spiritual fulfillment. Such consequences are clear when we look at the origin of such energies from ancient history.

The Pillars of Jachin and Boaz

The symbol for the sign of Gemini not only represents the twin powers of Castor and Pollux but also much older structures known as the twin pillars of Jachin and Boaz. These structures date back to the land of Egypt when, prior to the building of pyramids, pillars were considered to be a potent means of linking the worlds of gods and men.

Figure 13.1. Two pillars reaching into the sky,
memorializing the process of bringing heaven to earth
Mystical alchemical diagram of the Boaz and Jachin pillars of the
Temple of Jerusalem interpreted as cosmic principles, by Grant Schar, 1782

When the peoples of Lower and Upper Egypt decided to unify, each presented their own sacred pillar or divine connection to the union, agreeing they should be linked by a central beam and thus establish stability across the land. The right-hand pillar, Jachin, came from Lower Egypt and represented spiritual authority, while Upper Egypt contributed the left-hand pillar, Boaz, symbolizing physical strength and intellect. Together they created a doorway between the dimensions, facing east to meet the rising sun.

The central beam represented the goddess Ma'at, who symbolized righteousness, fairness, and justice. Such qualities arose from a place of detached compassion where her decisions always benefited the greatest number of people. It was clearly understood that the political stability and prosperity of a country was dependent upon the fair exchange of energy between these three aspects of the trinity, comprising the two pillars and the ever-evolving energy of the central beam.

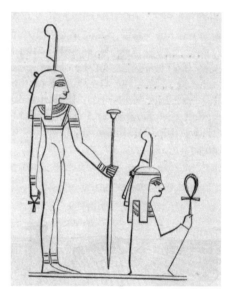

Figure 13.2. The goddess Ma'at, the dispassionate arbiter of justice

From E. A. Budge's *The Nile: Notes for Travellers in Egypt* (London: Harrison and Sons, 1902), pg. 189; under Wikimedia Commons license CC BY-SA 2.5

Over time the feminine connection uniting the twin pillars was lost and the crossbeam came to represent Yahweh, a storm god who united the kingdoms of Judah and Israel under the rule of King David and then King Solomon. With this change in the guardianship of the crossbeam, the unbiased authority that Ma'at embodied was lost and tight rules were developed to keep the general populace in a state of subservience. At the same time, the pillars took on more practical definitions. Strength (Boaz) was seen as a quality of the king and politicians who looked after defenses, law, and government, while establishment (Jachin) was the premise of the priests who managed religious righteousness.

In retrospect, it has become clear that without the central beam inspired by the archetype of the goddess Ma'at, our governance, as people of the world, can become a battle ground between church and state where both only seek to extend their own power. Perhaps it is time to restore a council of wise women to be our spiritual leaders, requiring them to make decisions that are worthy of the next seven generations and choosing only political and spiritual leaders who will fulfill this plan?

Let's take time now to practice a simple meditation to meet and master your own twin pillars.

As always make sure you are in a quiet and safe place where you are able to close your eyes; you may sit or lie down for this meditation.

Take a few deep breaths to quiet your mind, breathing out right down to your feet. Once you are settled in your body, move your awareness to your heart chakra, breathing in and out of this center, allowing the love of your soul to spread throughout your body.

Now, through your heart chakra, find yourself in a place in nature that you like to visit; it may be real or imaginary. You are then going to call toward you a spiritual animal that represents Jachin. The animal may be four legged, be two legged, be a creepy crawly, swim, or have wings. What animal appears? What three qualities describe this animal? For a few moments, step into this animal and feel the effect of embodying your spiritual power. Do you feel you have mastery over this animal or is it controlling you?

When you are ready, step clear of this animal and ask it to stand on your right-hand side. After centering yourself in your own being, repeat the process, calling toward you an animal that represents your kingly or physical power. What animal appears? What three qualities describe this animal? For a few moments, step into this animal and feel the effect of embodying your physical power. Do you feel you have mastery over this animal or is it controlling you? When you are ready, step clear of this animal and ask it to stand on your left-hand side.

Finally, reach out with your right and left hands so they rest on these two animals. With your body representing Ma'at, feel as their strengths both feed you and are fed by you when in harmony.

Bring your awareness back to the room where you are and open your eyes. Please make a note of your findings, remembering that if you weren't totally comfortable with the power of your animals, it is good to work with their energies every day until you feel you have mastery of these twin powers.

Grasping the Head of the Serpent

There is one final issue that needs to be addressed at this level. If we see these twin pillars as serpents of power that are vital to the building of our magician's wand, our hero must, metaphorically, be willing to grasp the heads of these two serpents in order to become master of these energies. A suitable analogy is the ability to pass a thread through the eye of a needle, a task only achieved by holding both items tightly. In anatomical terms, the eye of the needle is the vesica piscis–shaped passage in the diaphragm through which major vessels and the esophagus pass. Metaphysically, as our hero passes through this portal he graduates from service to the personality to service of the soul, transitioning from the ego-based solar plexus to the soul-based heart chakra.

If our hero fails to perform this task, his only source of power will come from emotional manipulation at the level of the solar plexus. Here his untamed serpentine energies will be allowed to thrash about wildly, spraying everybody in the vicinity like an unattended hosepipe. It is only by developing healthy emotional boundaries and choosing to own our power that we are truly able to call ourselves a hero.

14

CRONE—CANCER
Meeting Our Mirrors

Cancer

Alchemy: conjunction; recognizing and accepting the mirrors
of existence

Polarity: feminine; Crone, the sacred marriage of opposites

Moon Phase: gibbous; to improve and perfect

Now with the dual forces of physical strength and spiritual righteousness in his hands, our hero once again dives back into the Great Mother, attracting all manner of trials and tests similar to those faced by Odysseus in the *Iliad* and, more recently, by the courageous and wily Indiana Jones. While the hero would like to believe his mission is to rid the world of evil, battle to save the lives of the innocent, and win the hand of a beautiful woman, in truth many of the adversaries we meet in our lives are merely mirror images of our own hidden qualities, drawn into our awareness by the Great Mother in order to strengthen our inner core.

THE HAPPY CRAB

To understand this dynamic more closely and why we often try to avoid people who mirror the more difficult aspects of ourselves, let's explore the qualities of Cancer the crab. Those with strong aspects of

Cancer in their natal astrological chart will usually say to me, "I just want everybody to be happy." They love being at home surrounded by their extensive family, happily watching them get along with each other. But wearing their rose-colored glasses, Cancer individuals are usually the last to see that their marriage is on the rocks and their children are on drugs, constantly repeating to anybody who will listen: "We're such a happy, close-knit family."

When conflict does arise, the crab quickly scuttles off to hide under a rock or within the safety of their homelike shell. Unfortunately this approach does not allow for spiritual growth through the acceptance and integration of our mirrors but instead leads to denial, disassociation, and delusion. We may even choose to escape our own self-examination by judging as unacceptable anybody who carries the same traits we refuse to acknowledge.

I've seen this scenario played out on many occasions within the New Age or spiritual communities where "love and light" are sent out to those who carry so-called negative traits. Such "fluffy bunnies" often believe that they are too spiritually talented or evolved to need to do their own inner work, preferring to project onto everybody they meet their own untamed, dispossessed selves while saying, "Everybody I meet has the same issue; I wonder what is wrong with them?"

Thankfully, even though there will always be those who practice such spiritual bypass, the majority hear the wisdom of their soul and have the courage to turn and face their mirrors.

RESONATING WITH LOVE

How do we recognize our mirrors? As has already been mentioned, when we experience a strong emotional reaction to anybody—positive or negative—we are meeting a part of the self awaiting integration. When we admire someone, our aura starts to vibrate with excitement as the qualities expressed by our idol resonate with hidden qualities within us. By acknowledging this resonance, we can begin the journey toward full expression and integration of these particular aspects into our own life.

In the same way, when we meet someone who annoys us, our aura also vibrates but this time instead of calling it excitement we call it irritation. Instantly, like Cancer the crab, we move in two possible directions: either we try to hide from the offending energy or try to fix the individual with the problem. Our only goal is to do whatever it takes to reestablish our preferred state of harmony and happiness. We may even complain, "Why does that person always come and disturb my peace?"

But sadly, what we try to avoid will only make greater strides to attract our attention, shouting, "Mummy, I'm coming home to you!" Inevitably, the individuals who really get under our skin are our greatest teachers, commonly appearing as members of our immediate birth family. So when you feel irritated, resentful, or even fearful of someone you meet, please ask yourself:

- ◉ What three adjectives would I use to describe the behavior of that person?
- ◉ What judgments do I hold about people who behave in that way?
- ◉ Do I recognize those qualities in me?
- ◉ How difficult would it be for me to express those qualities in my life?
- ◉ What fears arise when I think of acting in that way?

These are not easy questions to answer and sometimes it's good to share your thoughts with a wise listener such as a therapist or good friend who knows you well. Here are some examples from my own life that may help you see the mirrors with greater ease.

In my life, I have always been seen as overly responsible, quickly jumping in to assist everybody I meet even when they were not asking for my help. Through the power of attraction, the people who really annoyed me in the past were those whom I considered irresponsible. Rather than accepting the mirror, my previous pattern was to apply all my energy to try to fix them so they could be just as heavily laden with responsibility as me!

Over time, I came to understand that the mirrors I feared facing were these:

1. Fear of being irresponsible and perhaps causing harm to others
2. Fear of being seen as a lazy and an invalid member of society
3. Fear of losing control and with it the belief that if I want a job well done, I have to do it myself
4. Fear of allowing someone else to take care of me

I wonder if you resonate with any of these fears? With the courage of the hero, I approached each fear in turn.

1. Through a series of events during my work as a hospital doctor, I came to see that it was arrogant to believe that someone's life was truly only in my hands: it's the soul that decides their future, not me.
2. I have taken a few sabbaticals from work, helping me get over the fear of being seen as invalid.
3. During these sabbaticals, I learned to accept that others are just as capable as me.
4. A serious illness gratefully persuaded me to allow others to take care of me.

As you see, some of these decisions I made willingly, while others were forced upon me by my soul. This is a common theme when acknowledging our mirrors, although I suggest that there are easier ways to approach this stage in our journey than to wait for a crisis to occur before accepting our dispossessed selves.

Here are some other questions to think about as you work to recognize your mirrors:

- If you see someone as selfish and narcissistic: how hard is it for you to stand up for yourself and take care of your own needs?
- If you judge someone for bragging about their achievements: what messages did you receive in childhood about celebrating yourself?
- If you are embarrassed by someone's outspoken nature: how difficult is it for you to speak the truth?

◉ If you criticize a woman for wearing sensually provocative clothes: how comfortable are you with your own sensuality?

Let's end this chapter by looking at a mythological story that shows that even goddesses can have problems accepting their mirrors.

Inanna is a young Sumerian maiden (soon to become queen) who lives on the bank of the Euphrates River.[1] *One day she sees a tree floating in the water; it has been uprooted by the wild southern winds. She takes the huluppu tree from the river and plants it in her sacred garden, longing for the moment when she can use its wood to create for herself a shining throne and a wonderful bed to lie upon.*

Ten years pass and the tree is still not ready for use. Then one day, Inanna is horrified to see that her precious tree has become the home of a serpent that cannot be tamed, who lives in the roots, and an owl-like bird, who nests in the branches—the Dark Goddess Lilith has made the tree her home. Inanna weeps!

Inanna calls upon her valiant mortal brother Gilgamesh, who cuts down the tree with his bronze ax, causing the serpent to slither away to the desert and the bird to fly to the mountains.

Inanna is delighted and fashions the now empty tree into her royal throne and bed.

Yet, as you may already know, merely cutting away the source of our discomfort does not mean it has disappeared from our life, because you cannot dismiss or forgive your own holographic creations. In Lilith, Inanna was meeting her untamed passions—the serpent—and her piercing insights—the owl—which we all meet as our psyche transitions from child through teenager to adult.

But Inanna was not ready to deal with these erratic and erotic feelings and instead destroyed the tree, relegating the essential parts of her creative psyche to the deeper recesses of her mind. Like many who follow her, she allows her brother's civilizing ax to cut away anything that does not conform to societal norms and to build her a structure where she can fit in.

Thankfully, as you see in a later chapter, Inanna is given other chances to integrate her dark goddess into her wholeness, opportunities that thankfully occur in our own lives. When you see a pattern repeat itself in your relationships, have the courage to stop and turn around to face the mirrors that will keep presenting themselves until we accept their message. As integration occurs, I promise you that your life will become richer, sweeter, and indeed happier.

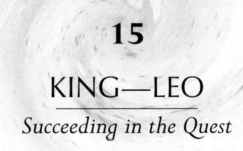

15

KING—LEO

Succeeding in the Quest

Leo

Alchemy: conjunction; the king is crowned
Polarity: masculine; king, success, pride, and celebration
Moon Phase: full; conscious integration and success

The crowning glory of the hero occurs when his dreams manifest into reality and, as a self-actualized being, he becomes sovereign of his own life. In mythology, the hero-king seizes the sword, wins the fair maiden, makes peace with his father, and takes the throne.

BUILDING SELF-ESTEEM

In our modern world, the prizes may be slightly different and include:

- Graduating from college or receiving a master's degree or Ph.D.
- Owning our first home
- Getting married
- Giving birth to our first child and taking on the mantle of parenthood
- Returning a healthy profit in our own business
- Publishing a first book

Whatever the success, the feelings are the same: elation, celebration, and pride. Yet for some, the moment of glory is diminished by self-deprecating beliefs—often passed down as family mottoes—that deny self-congratulation.

- Nobody likes a big head.
- Think of others, not just yourself.
- It is wrong or sinful to be full of pride.
- Remember that someone else did better.
- Your siblings are just as talented.
- Is that all? Let me tell you what *I* did . . .

Such sentiments are extremely detrimental to our search for wholeness and immortality. It is the strength and confidence of the king's ego and our ability to celebrate ourselves that provides us with the energy for the next stages of the journey, without which the descent into the underworld cannot take place. It intrigues me to find that every culture possesses a way of stealing personal power and making others feel small. In some countries it is known as the *tall poppy syndrome,* where we cut down or criticize anybody who thinks they are better than the rest. In Britain, we add healthy doses of cynicism and sarcasm: "You're going to do what?" or "Are you still spending time on that little hobby of yours; writing a book, I think you said?"

In the United States, the "put down" is fascinating. I start to tell a story about a recent achievement and the listener shows definite signs of interest, encouraging me to continue. Then at some point they interrupt and ask, "So what time of the day did you climb the mountain?" "Sunrise," I happily reply. "Oh," they say with a huge sigh, "You should have gone at sunset." And that's how it is done; stealing personal power from the hero turned king to make sure that nobody's successes are greater than your achievements. This is why finding ways to celebrate yourself that go beyond your culture's natural tide of discouragement are so important, especially in front of those whose own self-esteem is healthy enough not to need to steal your limelight.

THE LION KING

The perfect archetype of confident energy is seen in Leo the lion, king of the jungle. He gains respect from others, not only due to his physical strength and mighty roar, but from the way he strolls through the jungle with a self-assured air, knowing who he is and proud of his achievements.

I love being around people who have strong Leo energies in their astrological chart. They always seem to have thick, beautiful hair, and I watch as they run their hands through their mane or flick stray strands away from their face. Even if they have little or no hair, their hands are always touching their scalp. Leo, representing the sun, needs to be noticed, receive approval, and even spend time in the spotlight; otherwise such people can become dull and even depressed. It is fascinating to watch them work their magic in a room they have just entered. Their entrance is grand; they make jokes, often at their own expense, and are the first to volunteer when there is audience participation.

But don't be fooled by this bravado; there is often an insecure lion hiding in the depths, desperate to receive glowing accolades of approval. The more they try to please others, the more they are in need of acknowledgment. But as often happens with someone with low self-esteem from childhood, even though they are showered with appreciation, they seem to have a spigot at the bottom of their collection vessel that allows all this goodness just to drain away.

The lesson from Leo the lion is that we can never receive enough approval from outside ourselves to make us feel confident: it has to come from within. Celebrating our achievements and standing present in the full bloom of our successes is vitally important, for in doing so, we are also honoring the Great Mother. We have accomplished a creative miracle in her name, transforming a dream into reality and bringing her spiritual blueprint to life. This is a moment to celebrate, remembering that simple gratitude for divine assistance is not enough, for it often masks the belief "I don't deserve this," or conversely, "Look at me, I'm the favored one."

I like to celebrate myself at the end of every month, just before the new moon. Others may wish to do this at the end of a week while sitting with friends and family, where everybody nods approvingly, without stealing the limelight with their stories! I stand with my hand on my heart chakra and say out loud: "I bring to my heart this celebration . . . " and then name it. I know that when I embrace the fruits of my endeavors, the core of my being is made stronger and nobody can ever take this feeling away from me. When I celebrate myself, I'm also celebrating the love of the Great Mother and I hear the universe rejoice.

As king-queen, I suggest you ask yourself these questions and then celebrate:

- What three successes am I proud to say I developed from a seed, idea, or dream and nurtured into reality?
- Which dream did I almost not follow through on due to fear or lack of confidence?
- What or who made me continue with this dream despite the obstacles?
- Which moment gave me the greatest sense of satisfaction after I nurtured this challenging dream into reality?
- Who have been my greatest cheerleaders?
- What inner gift or talent keeps me going when things are tough? For example, humor, courage, curiosity, determination, an "I'll show them" attitude, or self-love.
- What have been my greatest successes, even though the amount of effort I expended and the decisions I had to make may not have been appreciated by anybody else? For example, staying in a difficult marriage, making choices about how to handle a child with drug addictions, or giving up my baby after birth.
- Which of my successes do I consider were most satisfying for my soul?

It is a wonderful experience for families to share their celebrations, recognizing this is one of the richest offerings we can give each other. When we hold ourselves in a healthy state of self-confidence, we encourage others to do the same and thereby pass this gift to subsequent generations.

That being said, the following story reminds us how easy it is for an ancestral message to become distorted in its telling until its truth is almost lost.

There was a beautiful old priory where ancient religious scripts were held and updated from time to time to accommodate the language of the day. The scribe chosen as translator was greatly honored to be picked because he was selected from a distinguished group of keen and devout priests.

Descending into the vault, he would work all day, ascending from the musty tomb only to sleep. One day the scribe failed to return to the surface, causing much concern among his colleagues. As they made their way down the cold stone steps, they heard crying coming from the vault below.

Moving quickly, they found the distinguished scholar in tears, surrounded by many aged books. "What's wrong?" they asked in dismay.

Through his tears the priest replied: "He didn't say celibate, *he said* celebrate!*"*

As we move forward, let's look at progress we've made toward the creation of our magician's wand. As we journeyed from Aries to Leo, we also traveled from the base chakra to the crown chakra where our king-queen is now celebrated. This can be equated to the in-breath or inspiration, breathing a dream into existence. In esoteric terms, we have created a strand of energy along our spinal cord known as the *ida*. Now the first length of the magician's wand is complete, and the hero turned king has every right to be pleased with himself and, like the mighty lion, can roar with pride. Success is complete—but fulfillment is another story, as the following chapters will reveal.

16

VIRGIN/TRIPLE GODDESS— VIRGO

And Then One Day . . .

Virgo

Alchemy: putrefaction and fermentation

Polarity: feminine; virgin aspect of the Triple Goddess, the vesica piscis

Moon Phase: disseminating gibbous; to distribute and convey

After all the excitement, it's time to reflect on the next stage of our journey, expiration, rededicating ourselves to our mission: to feed the Great Mother's heart with the gems of wisdom from our stories or experiences in order to expand her consciousness.

Having successfully completed the journey from the boy-child at the base chakra, through the hero at the solar plexus, to the king at the crown chakra, the next three phases of the journey represent the movement of energy from the crown chakra back down to the base chakra again. As we courageously descend, we will eat through and absorb the flesh of our experiences, and hence create the second length of our magician's wand, the *pingala*. This apparently destructive force, in opposition to the energy of growth that saw the boy crowned king, brings about the necessary tension for the development of the third strand of energy, the *sushumna,* and the extraction of the elixir of life.

Once again, we are not alone as the gods and the goddesses from ancient times have paved the way for us to follow.

As queen of Sumeria, Inanna has everything: two children, a husband, people to rule, and wealth beyond her dreams, and yet one day she hears the call from the great below, the underworld, and knows it is time.[1] She abandons her temples and responsibilities and prepares for her descent, gathering together seven of her most precious ornaments of status to take with her. She instructs her faithful servant Ninshubur that if her mistress doesn't return, she should ask for help. Inanna then begins her journey of descent into the darkness, which is the home of her unloved sister, Ereshkigal, a dark goddess or crone aspect of the Triple Goddess.

When she reaches the outer gates, she is met by Neti, the gatekeeper, who asks why she is on a road from which no traveler returns. Inanna replies that she has heard that Ereshkigal's husband, Gugalanna, has died and she wishes to witness the funeral rites. Hearing this, Ereshkigal, the dark sister, allows her to enter but commands Neti to take a piece of Inanna's royal garment from her at each of the seven gates or portals that Inanna encounters during the descent. "Let the holy priestess of heaven bow low," demands Ereshkigal.

And so starts Inanna's descent into the underworld.

So what is the impetus that causes Inanna to abandon her comfortable life and begin her journey into the underworld? She is listening to her intuition, which speaks to her from the depth of her soul, reminding her that the path to spiritual fulfillment cannot be measured merely by earthly success. At this time, the Virgin has created a vesical piscis–shaped portal into the other world or underworld, urging us to enter so we may know ourselves fully.

INTROSPECTIVE VIRGO

Each of us will take a number of journeys into the underworld during this lifetime. Similar to Inanna, the call to descend often arises from deep within our soul, entreating us to look beyond the glamour and

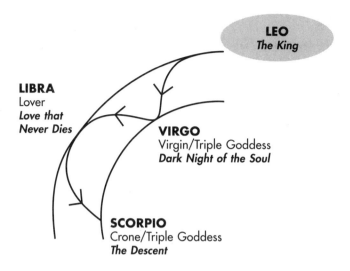

Figure 16.1. The three levels of descent
Image by Sherrie Frank

success of the king-queen and enter the darker domain of the Triple Goddess to fulfill our true spiritual destiny. Yet, as we were taught in Samudra Manthan, focused concentration and willpower are not sufficient to sustain our quest. We must equip ourselves with the energy of the turtle, turning our senses inward by practicing contemplation and introspection.

These qualities are to be found in the sign of Virgo, represented by a

Figure 16.2. The turtle, the primal mother
Drawing by Jessie Wilcox Smith, 1916

lady in white—the Virgin—with her arms wide open who says, "I have nothing to hide; I love and accept everything that exists within me." This compassion for even the most unlovable parts of the self is the purest quality expressed through the sign of Virgo. Her more challenging qualities reveal an obsession to create such perfect beauty by noticing small incidences of imperfection. These include paintings that are not hanging straight on a wall or the label of a shirt showing beyond the collar. Individuals with Virgo tendencies cannot resist the temptation to adjust the paintings or tuck the label in, even for a complete stranger. Their need to criticize or refine imperfection often drives them and everyone around them crazy.

The sign is ruled by the planet Mercury, causing those with strong energies of Virgo to spend a lot of time in their heads overanalyzing past interactions: "Why did I do that?" "What if I had taken another route?" "Why did they make me go in that direction?" "I hate them and I hate myself." Virgo can be hypercritical of others, but in truth, they are always harder on themselves, with high standards and multiple expectations as to how they should act and appear in the world.

The Virgin, as Virgo, offers these suggestions as we begin our descent into the underworld:

- ◉ Find compassion for yourself every day in small ways, especially when you make mistakes.
- ◉ Rather than taking the problem to your head for analysis, keep your awareness in your body by turning on music, dancing, singing, or even talking things out with a friend.
- ◉ Remember that it is most unlikely that any thoughts in your head will give you a positive and pleasurable lift if there is a tendency toward self-deprecation. Stay in the body.
- ◉ Find ways to kindly laugh at yourself, releasing any feelings of failure.
- ◉ Remember that you are loved and held dearly in the heart of the Great Mother.
- ◉ Turn that critical mind to one of discernment, ready to cut away anything that is not in harmony with your soul's journey.

THE DARK NIGHT OF THE SOUL

Sometimes our need to descend will appear when children leave home or when we reach the goal of success but find it lacks a sense of true fulfillment. At other times, we're pushed into the descent by a crisis such as a job loss, the death of a loved one, an illness, or divorce. Frequently, however, a dark night of the soul arises from nowhere, appearing to an outsider as if it has arrived as a bolt out of the blue, and yet there is no question that we will not accept its invitation.

We may find that it is not friends and family who can offer support during our descent, for they are often too invested in maintaining the present status quo and prefer we do not rock the boat. In my own experiences, it has been apparent strangers that held out a hand to me, saying, "Keep going; it's going to be alright." I suspect these human angels were sent to me by those who love me from the world of spirit. Of course, there is one other faithful friend that never abandons us: our soul, represented by Inanna's Ninshubur, who knows the importance of the journey and promises to be our guiding light as we descend.

Sadly, little is taught about this second phase of our spiritual growth, the phase of expiration. Often accompanied by loss of enthusiasm, sadness, depression, dispiritedness, and feelings of being dead inside, the immediate response by many within the medical profession is to prescribe "happy pills," often in an attempt to shut out their own fears concerning a descent into the underworld. In truth, many doctors and therapists are not educated to watch someone disintegrate or even die, with training focused on fixing the problem even at the cost of reducing the patient's quality of life. It is always clear to me those health professionals who have been through their own dark nights of the soul and those who have only read about that descent.

Physically, it is not uncommon to feel like a coiled spring that cannot take any more. This may be expressed as pain in the muscles and joints, headaches, indigestion, temperature fluctuations, palpitations, panic attacks, and severe mood swings. Many modern diseases, including Lyme disease, fibromyalgia, chronic fatigue syndrome, endocrine imbalances, and other immune-based illnesses often reflect a discon-nection from our soul's path. At these times, the Virgin's presence is even stronger, urging us to let go of old expectations and beliefs and trust her love and wisdom.

This is a good time to look at your own experiences:

- ◉ What events in your life caused you to become introspective and withdraw from the outside world?
- ◉ Who offered you the greatest support during your descent into the underworld?
- ◉ What did you need from your supporters during these times?
- ◉ Even though your known life was in chaos, what brought you comfort and the courage to keep going?
- ◉ Did you begin any new activities, such as art or meditation, during these times?
- ◉ What signs appeared that reassured you that you were emerging from the darkness?
- ◉ What advice would you give to anybody else going through the same experience?

In the end, it is our ability to surrender to the radiant embrace of the Virgin—the expression of the sign of Virgo—that propels us for-ward, for we know there is only one way to go: back to the heart of the Great Mother. As we turn away from the external source of suc-cess and enter the stillness of introspection and contemplation, we pass through the Virgin's vesica piscis, or yoni, ready to meet ourselves in the darkness.

17

LOVER—LIBRA

The Love That Knows No End

Libra

Alchemy: putrefaction and fermentation

Polarity: masculine; lover, compassion, courage,
self-discipline

Moon Phase: disseminating gibbous; to distribute and convey

It may seem strange that the phase of the journey related to love is masculine, associated as it is with the sign of Libra, the symbol of balance and harmony. Yet the love expressed in the following stories is dynamic and carries all the hallmarks of courageous acts that are symbolically associated with profound heroism. Indeed, it is the eternal embrace of our soul and the Great Mother's love that give us the courage to descend into the underworld in search of those parts of the self that have become separated.

LIBRA, THE LOVER OF HARMONY

Libra is represented by the symbol of the scales, reflecting the importance of balance and beauty in the lives of those with strong Libran tendencies in their astrological chart. Seen as the mediator, diplomat, bridge builder, and peace maker in any setting, it is easy to live with a Libran until they have to make a decision: "I don't mind what we do." "Whatever is good for you is good for me." They think they're being helpful when in fact their procrastination can become extremely frustrating.

The problem is that Librans need relationships and will do everything they can to make sure the relationship remains harmonic, avoiding conflict at all costs. To achieve this, the Libran individual spends much of their day thinking and worrying about the needs of others while ignoring what they need to maintain their own sense of balance. Asked to make a decision, they will often give you a detailed explanation as to why they cannot move until everyone else is happy, reeling off other people's personal stories to convince you that they are not procrastinating but just being considerate.

But do not make the mistake of seeing them as weak; their passion and love for anybody they consider important in their lives will see them tenaciously fight for that individual even at a cost to themselves. This determination and fierce love are summarized in the following stories of Demeter and Isis, two of the greatest goddesses in ancient history.

DEMETER

One of the best-known mythological stories associated with love concerns the goddess Demeter. Her grief for the loss of her daughter Kore and the subsequent trials to ensure her daughter's safe return are told in detail in the *Homeric Hymn to Demeter*, written around the seventh century BCE. You may have heard that Persephone was Demeter's daughter. Yet since Persephone is a Triple Goddess, the name of her virgin aspect is Kore while the crone aspect is known as Persephone.

Zeus, ruler of all gods and men, secretly promises Kore, his daughter, to his brother Hades, god of the underworld. Subsequently, Kore is abducted while innocently picking flowers and taken into Hades' underworld abode. According to the Greek version, we hear little more of Kore's plight until one year later. However, the Roman version of the story adds the suggestion that she was raped, in accordance with the dominant influence of the masculine energy prevalent in the culture at that time.

Meanwhile, on the surface, Demeter is beside herself with worry, entreating immortals and mortals alike to share what they know—and yet all are silent. Even though Helios, the sun god, and Hecate, the moon goddess, heard Kore's cries, they say nothing to her mother. For nine days Demeter flies around the world, refusing food, drink, and sleep until her daughter is returned. On the tenth day, Hecate comes forward and tells of the plotting between the brothers, and how Hades plans to make Kore his wife. Naturally, Demeter is livid and demands action from Zeus, who merely turns his back on her.

In revenge, she immediately withdraws all the nurturing energy from the Earth and begins to wander aimlessly among mortals, concealing her goddess powers and appearing as an old woman. Then one day she meets the four daughters of Keleos, the king of Eleusis, beside the city's well. Still hiding her divine light, she agrees to become nursemaid to the royal household, taking care of their infant brother, Demophon. She decides to secretly offer immortality to this royal child—having lost her own child—by feeding him the ambrosia of the gods, the nectar of eternal life. His parents marvel at how well he looks and yet are unaware of the reason.

Then one night, the queen walks in on Demeter as she attempts to confer eternal life on the child and, thinking that her nursemaid is trying to kill her son, shrieks. It is then that Demeter reveals herself as a golden-headed goddess and admonishes the queen for preventing her son from becoming immortal. She declares that from this day forward, every year the sons of Eleusis will be involved in a terrible battle. Yet she comforts the queen by saying, "Build me a temple and I will teach you the secrets and sacred rituals of immortality that will ease your pain."

Thus the Eleusinian mysteries were born (in approximately 1500 BCE) in Eleusis, Greece. They took place annually for almost two thousand years, with extreme secrecy surrounding what actually occurred during those nine days. What is known is that much of ceremony reenacted Demeter's fierce love as she searched for her daughter, with the climax being the vision of a fiery light that symbolized the presence of life after death.

Returning to the story:

The land has been barren for almost a year, and despite various entreaties, Demeter still refuses to restore the Earth's vitality until her daughter is returned. Zeus sends her all manner of envoys laden with gifts, but she refuses to relent. Finally, he concedes and sends Hermes, the messenger of the gods, into the underworld to bring back Kore, although by now she has become Persephone, queen of the underworld.

Hades, unwilling to give up his consort so easily, offers Persephone seeds from the pomegranate to sustain her on the journey back to the surface. Eager to return home and despite her mother's previous warnings to avoid any food from the underworld lest she become entrapped, Persephone eats the seeds. On the surface once again, Demeter is delighted to see her daughter but realizes Hades did not let her go without conditions. She knows that having eaten the seeds, her daughter is destined always to return to the underworld for at least one third of the year, signified by the darkness of winter. During this darkness, the Great Mother withdraws her energy from the Earth, replaying her grief for her lost daughter until she can once again rejoice at her return. At this time, she showers the Earth with spring's abundance of color and beauty.

Figure 17.1. The pomegranate, a potent symbol
of death and rebirth

This story exemplifies the deep resolution it takes to leave behind experiences that only give superficial satisfaction and enter the unknown world to search for what is precious to our heart. I wonder if you can recall times in your life when you have stepped out in search of something more meaningful and closer to your heart. This is a good time to reflect on these questions:

⊙ Can you remember a time in your life when you felt that the only thing that mattered was to stop and take time to reassess your life? (There may be many memories, but let's focus on one occasion.)

⊙ What would you say was the driving force behind this decision?

⊙ Can you pinpoint the source of the yearning for change? Were you driven by thoughts, emotions, body sensations, or something deeper, such as the pulse of your soul?

⊙ Do you remember any significant dreams around that time?

⊙ Did this reassessment coincide with a particular event, such as illness, death of a loved one, or divorce?

⊙ What was the reaction of those around you to your decision to make changes?

⊙ Did you feel the presence of any spiritual or divine love during this time?

⊙ In retrospect, how did this journey of love change your life?

ISIS

When we speak of the theme of love in mythology, our attention also turns naturally toward another goddess, the Egyptian goddess Isis and her great love for her brother-husband Osiris. Isis is also a Triple Goddess, expressing the power of creation as the goddess of fertility, motherhood, and magic. As the personification of the throne, her original headdress symbolized an open seat. This denoted the fact that all pharaohs had to humbly come and sit in her lap in order to gain the power to rule, a prerequisite set by many of the sovereign or Mother goddesses.

Figure 17.2. Isis, the Great Mother

Isis suckling Horus, from *History of Rome, and of the Roman People,*
From Its Origin to the Invasion of the Barbarians by Victor Duruy
(Boston: C. F. Jewett, 1883)

The Grief of Isis over the Death of Osiris

Osiris and Isis rule Egypt harmoniously, bringing justice and civilization to all their people. Yet Osiris has a bitter and jealous brother, Set or Seth, who seeks to take the throne for himself. Through his scheming, he creates a beautifully decorated sarcophagus that is exactly contoured to the frame of Osiris. Set then invites everyone to a magnificent feast during which he offers a gift to anybody who can fit comfortably in the box. Osiris, who is pure of heart, suspects nothing and eagerly steps inside the sarcophagus and lies down. Immediately, the lid is shut and nailed closed with molten lead poured into the seam to seal his fate. The tomb of Osiris is then thrown into the Nile River, where it awaits discovery by his beloved wife, Isis.

Isis is distraught and begins to search for her beloved. She comes across the box lodged in a tamarisk bush and immediately rises up from the ground as a hawk, singing the song of mourning. As she soars above the Earth, she casts a spell that allows the spirit of the dead Osiris to enter her. Hence she conceives and bears a son, Horus, whose destiny is to avenge his father's death. Scared that the uncle Set may try to kill her son, Isis hides him on an island and returns to Thoth, the lord of knowledge, to obtain the magic necessary to bring her beloved back to life.

However, before this can happen, Set discovers Osiris's dead body and, determined to finish his life once and for all, cuts the body into fourteen pieces, scattering them across the land of Egypt. Yet Isis's love does not diminish. She starts to collect the pieces, erecting a temple to Osiris at the location where each piece is discovered.

Eventually, Osiris is sewn together and his spirit is returned to his body. But because he is dead, he cannot return to the living and hence descends to Amenti, the place of the dead, and becomes its lord.

The temples Isis erects represent the acceptance into our heart of every piece of the self, without judgment or favor, just as the Great Mother loves every one of us unconditionally.

THE POWER OF LOVE

The common theme of this story and the story of Demeter is the amazing capacity to love shown by these powerful Mother archetypes, reminding us that even in our darkest moments we are never alone and that we too possess such love. As humans, we often go through some very difficult situations, and yet there is a determination to survive based not on mere physical strength but a deep soul love that never dies. Sometimes we become overwhelmed by the emotional pain of loving, but a wise Maori healer once told me, "When the pain becomes too unbearable, offer it into the heart of the Great Mother, knowing her heart is large enough to embrace and transform anything that has become a burden too heavy to carry."

18

CRONE/TRIPLE GODDESS— SCORPIO

The Descent

Scorpio

Alchemy: putrefaction and fermentation

Polarity: feminine; crone aspect of the Triple Goddess, death and chaos

Moon Phase: last or third quarter; to revise and reevaluate

This stage of the journey is associated with the sign of Scorpio—the scorpion—often depicted as intense, dangerous, deep, sexual, and with an interest in the occult, wonderful descriptors of crones such as Inanna's sister, Ereshkigal.

Let's continue their story:

As Inanna begins her descent into her sister's abode, she is instructed to give up a piece of her royal garment at each of the seven gates she will encounter during her descent. "Let the holy priestess of heaven bow low," demands Ereshkigal.

Following his mistress's command, Neti, the gatekeeper, opens the outer gate and allows Inanna to enter, but only after he has taken the shugurra, or crown of the steppe, from her head. Inanna demands to know what is happening, but Neti simply states, "The ways of the underworld are perfect

and are not to be questioned." Inanna's descent continues. At each gate another piece of her clothing or a piece of jewelry is taken, and each time she asks the same question and receives the same answer.

As Inanna stands naked before Ereshkigal, the latter looks at her with the eye of death, speaks words of wrath, utters a cry of guilt, and kills her. Then Inanna's corpse is hung on a hook on the wall as if it is a piece of rotting meat.[1]

Enter the Crone, who loves us so much she will almost destroy us to ensure that our inner light shines. There is no avoiding her fiery cauldron if we are truly committed to entering the domain of the Great Mother and merging with her eternal oneness. Yet, as you can see, this is the most challenging of all the phases of the journey, directed as it is by a dark goddess such as Ereshkigal.

Yet some people do try to avoid stepping into her cauldron, making excuses such as:

- I'm too busy right now. Can you come back later?
- I'm fine, thank you. I don't need your help, as I'm taking lots of vitamins and hormones to stay permanently youthful.
- I think you're looking for the wrong person. Yes, I'm depressed and miserable, but I like it this way. Being depressed must be better than jumping into a cauldron!
- I have found a shortcut to transformation that avoids the messy business of death.

The Crone, however, is not a lady to be ignored. As the keeper of time, she gives us notice that the psychological defenses of denial and projection will no longer suffice. They will not be strong enough to deflect her energies as she rises up to bring about the necessary transition of the old world to make way for the new.

Already we may be seeing her influence, as old grievances, betrayals, abuses, and hatred are being forced from their uneasy resting place within the ground, to be acknowledged and transformed in ways that will lead to lasting peace. In this new world of ether, there is no place for secrets, for *What you do to me, you do to yourself. All is known, nothing is hidden, for you and I are one.*

THE SCORPION

As mentioned at the beginning of this chapter, unlike its mild mannered and happy, watery sister Cancer, Scorpio rules deep and murky waters, where hidden dangers lurk. Those with strong aspects of Scorpio in their astrological chart are often described as intense, sensual, and determined, fearlessly entering places where death, the occult, abuse, and danger abound. In fact, due to their strong association with the Crone, they usually have no personal fear of death.

They do possess a stinger, but unhappily for the Scorpions it is commonly they who are stung. This is because once they get their teeth into something, they will not let go. Their greatest joy is to assist in the transformation of everyone they meet. "Hallo," they say as they enter a room, "why don't you just jump into my cauldron, and my intense heat will melt the meat from your bones." Naturally, but to their surprise, people tend to run the other way. "Stop," Scorpions shout, "I'm only trying to help."

Unfortunately, probably due to living in murky waters too long, they are often short sighted when it comes to saving others. They will happily jump into the ocean and even give over their own lifejacket if they see someone drowning. Almost too late they realize that they are going to drown, pulled down by the weight of the emotional sadness of other people. Their other blind spot is an inability to see that a relationship has come to the end, their motto being "When things don't work, it's time for me to try harder." And that is why they eventually feel the pain of being stung by their own venom as they reluctantly admit the relationship is dead but fail to release their stinger. Scorpio, of all the signs, has a vicious memory, holding on to old bitter emotions for years; forgiving but never forgetting!

ENTERING THE CAULDRON

Today, the Dark Goddess is demanding we take ownership of all of our creations, reconnecting to subpersonalities or parts of our soul that are trapped in stories from the past. These aspects of the self are crying out for attention and will not be quiet until we accept them into our heart. Such cries for help may come through illness, relationship difficulties, or an intense reaction to events outside us that represent subpersonalities hidden in the darkness. For instance, we may become upset by stories that speak of:

- A child being neglected or abused: where is that abused child hidden in us?
- A woman who has no voice: where have we lost our voice?
- A man or woman abusing their power: where does that abuser live inside us?
- A man or woman who feels ostracized: what part of us has been abandoned?
- A person whose pain and rage makes them want to kill: where is that pain in us?

Another way that these lost parts can gain our attention is by using the captured emotions from past events to repeatedly recreate scenarios that are echoes of the origin event. So when we say "This always happens to me" or "My husband's energy is just like my mother's energy," it is true. Because as mighty creative beings and creators of our reality, we know there is no event in our life—however traumatic—that doesn't offer the opportunity for growth and learning for the soul through the extraction of gems of wisdom. So we cleverly recreate stories in order to collect those precious gems and bring the lost parts of ourselves into our heart. An alternative to the hypothesis I have just presented is to believe that we are mere victims to our lives and that life just happens and that, without free will, we are powerless to change anything. I can't accept the second scenario to be true.

But even if you suffer from a little bit of victimhood, never fear, the Crone is here to help us, eager to strip the meat from the bones of our stories in her fiery cauldron so we may know ourselves fully. Her methods may be crude and demanding but the truth is *she loves us so much; she refuses to let us be less than we are.*

To speed up the process it's helpful to ask ourselves the following questions:

- From what story in my past do I still hold feelings of anger or sadness?
- If I were to watch a video of this event, where would I stop the video to expose the most impactful memories?
- What aspect of the scene is most painful?
- What part of the self—subpersonality—carries this pain? Is it also held in a specific part of my body?
- What part of me did I need to abandon or reject many years ago, because I could not have survived while carrying this part of the self? For example, the crying, demanding, or innocent child.
- Did I ever meet and then abandon powerful and even destructive subpersonalities as they were felt to be unacceptable in my well-ordered life?
- Are there other aspects of the soul that I rejected and abandoned through judgment, whether from myself or others?
- Am I ready to return to these stories, listen to the subpersonalities lost in the shadows, and embrace them into my heart?
- What gems of wisdom are ready to be extracted from my experiences to add to the Great Mother's pool of consciousness?

Only when we burn away the story and get down to the bones of the event can we then extract gems of wisdom that become golden nuggets of wisdom that are not right or wrong but just the truth.

Under the loving guidance of the Crone, are you ready to descend into your own inner basement or cellar and break open the seals on all those storage chests and old boxes that have been collecting dust, not only during this life but for many lifetimes? Most of these sealed boxes have been moved from house to house (life to life), unopened and untouched, saturated in the fear of what may be unleashed should the contents ever see the light of day.

It takes great courage to accept into our heart a part of us that is considered dark or destructive and yet, without total acceptance of both our light and dark personas, we will never know immortality in the heart of the Great Mother.

Once we accept that we are ready to release the burden of carrying our heavy baggage, our "house" feels lighter. We know that as we unearth the true treasures contained within, our Ka, or light body, becomes stronger and brighter.

THE SEXUAL FIRES OF PURIFICATION

As you can imagine, the words *putrefaction* and *fermentation* are not the most enticing advertisements for transformation. So years ago this process was renamed sex. In its highest form, love making, this sacred process brings an individual face to face with their eternal and perfected form by passing them through sexual fires of purification, transforming them from their base state of duality into their ecstatic state of illumination.

To aid this process, many ancient cultures trained priestesses to perform sacred sexual rituals. Through the burning away of the non-essential energies linked to the ego, altered states of consciousness were achieved both by the priestess and those in her company. These women, such as the priestesses of Isis, had as their symbol the serpent and were revered for their mastery of their sexual fires. Through their training, they came to honor and respect the powerful serpentine energy that runs along the spine, linking the chakras. They knew that when this serpentine ladder is activated, such as during sexual intercourse, a state of orgasmic bliss is ultimately reached as unification with the Great Mother is achieved. Through management of the breath, refinement of the subtle energies found within each chakra, their ability to generate serpent power within their womb, and a healthy relationship between their physical and spiritual worlds, these priestesses became a magnetic vessel of fire for the purification and transformation of any soul who came into their presence.

Sadly, over time, the patriarchy found it demeaning for men to require the services of women to connect to their own divine nature. They therefore cast out the sacred priestesses—the true meaning of the terms *harlot* or *scarlet woman*—to the edges of society. Today they are returning, not carrying their heads in shame but in joyful celebration of the sexuality and sensuality of the female body.

THE LABYRINTH

There is one design, found within many cultures, that creates the pathway for the descent into the underworld: the labyrinth, a unicursal maze with one way in and one way out. Most traditions see the labyrinth as representing the sacred tomb/womb of Mother Earth where the crone goddess—similar to Ereshkigal—waits patiently at its center. Traditionally, labyrinths were guarded by women, for only they were acknowledged to understand the principles behind the cycles of death and rebirth.

Some of the earliest examples of a labyrinth date back to around 5000 BCE and were built in Mesopotamia in honor of Inanna. The Hopi liken the labyrinth to their *kiva,* or underground sanctuary, from which they believe they are reborn from the underworld. In southern India, Hindu women mark their homes with the sign of the labyrinth at the beginning of the decline of the sun at the summer solstice.

The best-known tale concerning the labyrinth is that of the Minoan hero Theseus, who enters the labyrinth with the aid of Ariadne's thread to meet and kill the Minotaur, who is half man and half bull. The retelling of the story, however, often fails to include the fact that Ariadne was a powerful moon goddess and was helping Theseus to engage with his own inner demon, the Minotaur. The story ends with Theseus celebrating his success without acknowledging the help he received from Ariadne, whom he then carelessly abandons; probably not his wisest move!

The classic design of a labyrinth has seven circuits or paths that

Figure 18.1. The design of a typical Cretan labyrinth

represent the seven chakras or portals of consciousness along which we must descend to reach the center. Having died to our old self, new life is breathed into us and we return along these same paths until we emerge at the exit, reborn with new energy and purpose. Although many labyrinths today are built on flat land, there are a few built into a hill, such as the famous three-dimensional labyrinth that winds around Glastonbury Tor. As the pilgrim walks this seven-path labyrinth, he or she is given the opportunity to offer to the Great Mother those things that have become unnecessary baggage and enter, with a great sense of freedom, his or her own inner center at the top of the Tor. Finally, a labyrinth that was built in the twelfth century by the Knights Templar in Chartres cathedral, France, takes on a more complex shape, with four quadrants and a six-petalled rose at its center (see figure 18.2 on page 204). The cathedral is located on top of a hill where several ley or earth-energy lines intersect, leaving no doubt that its architects knew exactly what they were doing, given that this is a perfect portal into the underworld. Here the pilgrim would meet both the Virgin and the Crone, personified by the Black Madonna, in order to experience their own death and rebirth.

Figure 18.2. The design of the fabulous Chartres labyrinth,
the biggest church labyrinth built during the Middle Ages
By Ssolbergj, under Wikimedia Commons license CC BY-SA 3.0

To close this chapter, let's return to Ereshkigal and Inanna in the underworld.

When Inanna fails to reappear, her faithful servant (intuition) seeks the help of the gods. Only Enki, the wise one, offers a solution.[2] *From beneath his fingernails, he takes some dirt and fashions two little androgynous creatures,*

Kurgarra and Galatur. Because they are as small as flies, he believes they will not be seen by Ereshkigal's guards. He tells these creatures that when they enter her chamber they will see the Dark Goddess moaning and groaning as she is about to give birth. He advises them to mirror her moans, so when she says "Oh! Oh! My inside," they should say, "Oh! Oh! Your inside," and when she says, "Oh! Oh! My outside," they should say, "Oh! Oh! Your outside."

The two little creatures do as they are bid: When they are inside Ereshkigal's birth chamber, they mirror her cries. She is so amazed they are not frightened by how ugly she looks that she offers them a gift. They ask for Inanna's corpse, hanging on the hook. Once the body is in their care, they pour the juice of life upon it and Inanna returns to life.

These tiny asexual creatures fashioned from the basic component of life are devoid of an agenda or personal desire and thus are able to be completely present to the Dark Queen's distress, offering her unconditional compassion. Having spent most of her life hiding in the caverns of the underworld and fearful that her raw emotions will cause further alienation, she is amazed by their empathy and bestows upon them the gift of Inanna's rebirth.

It is this level of love that we are being asked to shower upon all faces of the self that have been shrouded in shame or fear. This only happens when we, like the small creatures, are willing to fully embody the wounded part of ourselves, feeling the full range of emotions inside such characters without judgment or the need to change who they are. In truth, *feeling does bring healing*. This is the most challenging part of our journey. Yet when we decide that it is no longer acceptable to hide or feel ashamed of any part of the self, we are truly free to be ourselves. This process into freedom is powerfully expressed in this poem by Thich Nhat Hanh, entitled "Please Call Me by My True Names."[3]

> *I am the twelve-year-old girl,*
> *refugee on a small boat,*
> *who throws herself into the ocean*

after being raped by a sea pirate.
And I am the pirate,
my heart not yet capable of seeing and loving.
. . .
Please call me by my true names,
so I can wake up
and the door of my heart
could be left open,
the door of compassion.

When we accept we are all children of the Great Mother unified in her heart, then we will truly know the meaning of forgiveness.

Namaste: I am another one of you.

19

SAGE—SAGITTARIUS
The Truth Shall Set Them Free

Sagittarius

Alchemy: the beginning of distillation

Polarity: masculine; sage

Moon Phase: last or third quarter; to revise and reevaluate

It is the sage or wise man within all of us, symbolized by the sign of Sagittarius, who can distinguish truth from illusion and gold from base metal. With detached compassion he meets each aspect of the self or

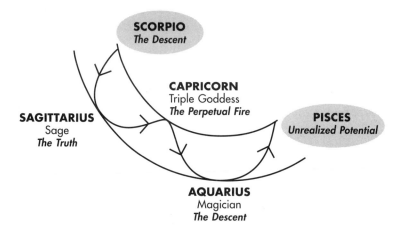

Figure 19.1. The final magic of the Triple Goddess

Image by Sherrie Frank

subpersonality as it emerges from the fire, seeking its authenticity rather than judging its worth. In alchemy, the completion of the process of fermentation is symbolized by the beautiful tail of the peacock. This reveals the many "eyes" of our subpersonalities that, liberated from the caverns of isolation and rejection, we proudly display for all to see.

EXPANDING INTO TRUTH

This stage of our journey is ruled by the archer, Sagittarius, who, half man and half horse, loves to travel far and wide in search of the truth, whether in his mind or physically. Indeed, there is nobody more restless in the zodiac than someone with strong Sagittarian energies. They can become easily annoyed by people who are unreasonable or tell lies and are not afraid to let them know how they feel and what is true. Indeed, it would be fair to say that sometimes the archer will fire their arrow before they think where it may land or speak before engaging their thoughts. Some may call them tactless, sarcastic, or opinionated, while a Sagittarian just believes they are right. Their ability to know what is true and what is not is uncanny and should be trusted.

SUBPERSONALITIES
HELD WITHIN OTHER LIVES

I'm often asked in my work whether someone has had a past life, and I reply with a laugh, "Many lives and often with the same theme." Even though we may know that our experiences are not linear—past, present, and future—it's hard for us to appreciate that we also have memories from future lives as our brain can only explain things that repeat themselves in our daily life or can be found on a search engine such as Google or Bing!

But for years science-fiction books, comics, movies, and games have been revealing to us potential technological breakthroughs that have now become our reality. Of course, we could ask, "Were these writers inspired by a glimpse into the future or did our fascination in these subjects cause a shift in the holographic matrix causing our dreams to become reality?" And that in a nutshell is the problem with those who search for the truth—there is no finite end to our journey.

Looking back ten years; could you have imagined that you would have been where you are now? What aspects of your life today would particularly surprise the younger you? The search for truth does not begin in the external world but with our willingness to follow a heartfelt dream or idea until we can realize its true value as a golden gem for our soul.

So rather than calling something a past life, I prefer to see all lives—past, present, and future—as just events around a certain archetypal subpersonality, like petals of a flower, in the center of which is the soul. Each of these events may have occurred in a different time or location but in truth, we merely design an appropriate backdrop for our story in order to create the right atmosphere for that particular subpersonality. Then we drop into the story and experience ourselves as that subpersonality.

The only problem is that when we fail to collect the gems of wisdom from that story and instead leave this Earth with a bagful of painful or angry emotions, we are setting ourselves up to use those emotions again as the source of energy that creates a future life, with the same subpersonality directing the show. In this way, we can experience the same petal many times until we have the courage to become introspective and

Figure 19.2. Flower with petals and the soul center

dive into the Crone's cauldron so we can accept this aspect of the self into our heart, extracting the gems of wisdom.

So when someone asks me whether they have ever been persecuted for their beliefs, my reply may be, "Not once but many times. The problem is," I add, "that you were so attached to the fact you wanted other people to agree with you that when they didn't, you often held on to your resentment, dying still full of anger. My advice: either decide to keep your thoughts to yourself or let go of your attachments with the satisfaction that you spoke your truth."

Past-life regression work is fascinating but should always move toward soul empowerment, embracing into the heart of all the subpersonalities hiding in the shadows. Throughout my life, I've met many such subpersonalities. On most occasions I didn't go in search of them; rather, they came to me, bringing enormous opportunities for growth and spiritual empowerment. Thus, over time, I have met myself in many forms:

- A happy Irish mother with eight children
- A Roman soldier who hangs himself, conflicted between his belief in Jesus's teachings and the orders given him by his superiors
- A black servant given his freedom
- A pioneering farmer exhausted and despairing of the continual rains that wash away the crops
- A brave Native American warrior devoted to his family and to the land
- A child who dies weighed down with responsibility as he defies the wishes of his parents and, while playing, falls into a pond and drowns
- A tyrant and soldier who treats everyone with contempt and who dies alone and in pain on the battlefield
- A female black magician who uses her skills to possess what is not hers to possess

As each character appeared to me, they brought with them an emotional quality that energized every cell of my body until I felt I *was* that subpersonality. Such embodiment invested in me a real sense of authenticity—the knowledge there was no meat or emotions left on the story with only the bones or truth remaining.

I'm not going to suggest this was an easy process, especially given that one of the characters possessed a cruel, cold, and calculating energy. I first became aware of this subpersonality when I became fearful of spending too much time in my lower three chakras, preventing me from feeling fully secure, nurtured, and confident. Initially, I offered this subpersonality love, in the hope it would then leave me alone, but it only sneered at me. "I am unaffected by your humanoid emotions," it said.

Oh dear, I thought. *What do I do now?*

Many weeks passed, and I was growing desperate, for, like Lilith in Inanna's tree, this energy seemed to have made my body its home. Calling out for help during a seminar, I was gifted with great advice: "Draw into your heart those parts of the self that cause distress and say to them: I accept you, as part of myself, into my heart." Immediately, as I spoke the words, the energy changed and the reptilian energy— for that is what it was—became absorbed into my heart. It then transformed into the pure essence of consciousness, judged as neither good nor bad, but rather as an essential part of my soul.

It is the role of the sage within us all to question our deepest intentions and beliefs until only the truth remains. Such a process is reflected in the story of Inanna's descent through the seven levels, gates, or chakras where she is asked to remove a different item of her identity before standing naked in the light of her own truth.

Our inner sage is asking us these same questions now:

◉ What is your true authority? This relates to the first gate, the crown chakra. Do you need a physical crown to claim sovereignty of your being? Are you truly sovereign—king or queen—of your own life? Do you need the approval or accolades of others to feel good about yourself?

It is only when we don't need the crown or approval from external success that we come to know our true authority.

◉ Are you ready to follow your inner sight or intuition? This relates to the second gate, the third eye, linked to clarity and detached wisdom or intuition. Do you trust your intuition? Can you clear your mind sufficiently to hear your inner guidance?

The ability to close our outer eyes and still trust our inner guidance is the true sign of an intuitive being.

◉ Can you let go of control and trust the outcome? This relates to the third gate and the throat chakra, the center that loves to know the outcome before making any decisions. Do you recognize the excuses you make or questions you continually ask to avoid change?

Surrendering to the love of our heart and allowing it to guide us releases us to enjoy the flow of the present moment. This is probably one of the hardest gates.

◉ What is left when there is only love? This relates to the fourth gate and the heart chakra. Without realizing it, true love is often hampered by conditions, expectations, demands, and desires. Can you release these and allow love in?

We are always marinated in the love of the Great Mother: there is nothing else.

◉ Who are you? This relates to the fifth gate and the solar plexus, the seat of our small ego. Can you stand tall and celebrate yourself without the need for approval or being affected by criticism?

Confidence is a state of being when the small ego and the soul are united as one.

◉ Why are you hiding? This relates to the sixth gate and sacral chakra. This gate is linked to our relationships and asks: Where are you hiding due to shame or humiliation? Where are you not respecting yourself?

There is no place for shame or secrets, as the Great Mother sees all parts of us and loves us even more.

◉ Do you belong to yourself? This relates to the seventh gate and base chakra. This final gate strips us of our last defenses until we are naked. It asks: Can you be secure in just being yourself?

The greatest security comes when we move beyond tribal rules and root ourselves in the fertile and eternal soil of Mother Earth. Then we know we are not alone but exist in the all-oneness.

As Inanna stands before Ereshkigal, the dark sister sees that Inanna is still wrapped in the skin of mortal "life," and with one stroke she removes the outer covering so the spirit can fly free.

20

TRIPLE GODDESS— CAPRICORN

The Perpetual Fire

Capricorn

Alchemy: distillation; the pelican
Polarity: feminine; the Triple Goddess
Moon Phase: balsamic; to distill and transform

Capricorn is one of the most complex signs of the zodiac and yet, astrologically, a Capricorn personality is often described in relatively simple terms as someone who is dutiful, responsible, loyal, pessimistic, and a lover of lists! But if we look at the glyph, the image is that of a fish-goat representing the archetype of an individual who can reach great heights as well and the depths of consciousness; in other words this person possesses the ability to experience wholeness or integration. With this understanding, I always see someone with strong energies of Capricorn within their natal astrological chart as someone expressing integrity.

It is believed that the symbol of the fish-goat represents an ancient group of beings—known as *the serpents of wisdom*—who came to this planet to impart wisdom and the knowledge of healing, mathematics, and science.[1] Their message was very clear: it is through our own disciplined inner work that integrity or wholeness is achieved.

Metaphysically, this is seen when we feed the fire of our heart with enough distilled gems of wisdom until our heart emits a constant light; our heart has become a perpetual fire.

For a deeper understanding of this process, let's turn our attention toward a small group of female fire keepers, the vestal virgins, whose job it was to keep the flames of the heart of the Roman Empire alight.

THE VESTAL VIRGINS

During the era of Roman civilization, six beautiful maidens were chosen to dedicate their lives to keeping the perpetual fire alight, acknowledged to be the mystical heart of the Empire. There were named after the Roman Goddess Vesta, the goddess of the hearth.

These young virgins received many privileges that were normally denied ordinary women. In return they were expected, on the pain of death, to focus all their attention on maintaining the fire, remaining unmarried, and being unavailable to any other distraction.

Why would such a powerful patriarchal society bestow so much

Figure 20.1. The vestal virgins,
tasked with keeping humanity's fire alive
"The Vestal Virgins" by Rudolf Cronau, 1919 in *Woman Triumphant*

importance on a group of girls? The vestal virgins were not merely fire keepers but, like their namesake, were also protectors of the hearth, considered to be the heart (heart-h) of the home or culture. The Romans knew the perpetual fire was the source of their continued prosperity and abundance and without it creativity would become stagnant, infertility would increase, the land would become barren, and the people would be depressed. In essence, their empire would not survive.

Most people today are still drawn to the warm glow of a fire, recognizing its ability to encourage a community spirit, rekindle dreams, and add a magical quality to stories told. Yet so many homes are built without a central hearth or communal cooking area, and somehow a microwave just doesn't have that same appeal! Hence we see people gravitating toward places where there are bright lights, such as malls or shopping centers, bonfires, and even around candles, in an attempt to experience the heart of the perpetual fire.

So what is so unique about a perpetual fire? During my research I came across this quote by the Sufi master Hazrat Inayat Khan, which helped to bring clarity to this important question:

> If love is pure [and] if the spark of love has begun to glow, then there is no need to go somewhere to gain spirituality, [for] spirituality is within. One must keep blowing the spark till it turns into a perpetual fire. The fire-worshippers of old did not worship a fire that went out, they worshipped a perpetual fire. Where is that perpetual fire to be found? In one's own heart.[2]

If the fire is within our own heart, then love is its fuel, especially when we equate love to a deep desire for connection. I know this to be true as one of the most common desires I hear in my work is people looking for love, a relationship, intimacy, and companionship and perhaps the feeling of joy that comes from connecting to something greater than ourselves. It is our heart that continually yearns for connection and our intuition that makes it happen. Sadly, I also meet people who have become so disconnected from their hearts through pain, fear, or shame that they now believe they are unlovable. Many diseases of the heart and immune system relate to such a loss of connection to the heart.

So how do we open our hearts to love? We begin in small ways, looking not for love but for joy, which is the fundamental energy of the heart. Every time we feel joy, we are making a connection to the Great Mother's heart, whether it is through a beautiful sunrise, the laughter of a child, or the sensations that come from being in the company of good friends. It's a good idea to keep a journal and each day make a note of moments of joy, however short.

THE MIRACULOUS HEART

To take our exploration of the perpetual fire to a deeper level, it is important to study the facts that are already known about a unique organ of the body: the heart.

The heart consists of a complex electromagnetic system that, with every beat, produces enough energy to power a small electric bulb. Its amplitude is forty to sixty times greater than that of brain waves. The field produced by this energy radiates out some twelve to fifteen feet beyond the body, with the most powerful part of the spectrum existing within the first three feet. It is no wonder we feel so good in the presence of someone who exudes heartfelt joy.

Research has shown that a single cell taken from a heart has an innate memory that allows it to continue to beat even when it removed from the body and disconnected from the nervous system. In time, it will start to fibrillate and then slowly die. Yet if we take two cells that are both fibrillating and bring them together, they will at some point connect energetically and both of them will be restored to normal health. If two unhealthy cells in a laboratory can respond in this way, just imagine the healing potential for two people whose hearts are open to each other, and then imagine what could happen to whole nations!

In another experiment, the fibrillating cell was brought into the presence of a healthy cell. Within minutes the healthy cell entrained the sick cell back to health, causing both to beat in harmony. This power of the heart cell to entrain another cell is based on the principle of congruency: each cell holds the memory of oneness. This is the way great healers bring healing to anybody in their presence; by radiating a strong state of harmony, unity, and congruence. In other words, it is far more potent to *be* the healing rather than *give* healing.

Perhaps this is a good time to ask ourselves some heartfelt questions:

- In the past week, what caused you to feel joy—even for just a few moments? Where in the body was the feeling strongest?
- If being *in joy* is important for our heart, are there areas of your life that are not enjoyable? Is there anything you can do to feed your heart with joy again?
- With whom do you feel most at peace and able to be yourself? If you cannot think of someone, could it be when you're in nature or with your pets?
- What makes your heart sing?
- Can you remember a time when you met someone whose energy was so peaceful and pure that you immediately felt calmer and more at peace with yourself?

THE HEART AND THE TORUS

It has now been shown that the electromagnetic energy of the heart takes the shape of a *torus* (a toroid shape)[3] that is in essence a three-dimensional vesica piscis (see figure 20.2). Geometrically, a torus is formed by rotating many circles around a tangential line, the center of which touches all the rotated circles exactly. There are three main torus shapes, the most common being similar to a ring doughnut: a tube torus.

We now know there are many examples of tori in our world, and all have the ability to communicate with each other directly:

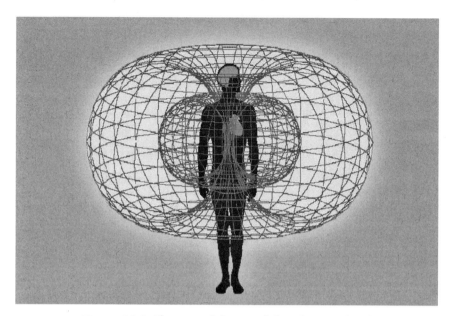

Figure 20.2. The sacred design of the tube torus and
the toroidal field of the heart

- **The atom:** The movement of the particles within the atom is toroidal.
- **DNA:** The double helix is known to act as a torus, transforming energy and information into and out of the DNA.
- **A chakra:** The energy of the torus appears as swirling chalices radiating out of the front and back of the body, with energy flowing in and out of both chalices.
- **The electromagnetic field of the body:** Energy pours into and out of the crown and base chakras, the spine acting as the central axis.
- **The Tree of Life:** The roots and the branches exist at opposite ends of the axis.
- **The Earth:** The magnetic field surrounding the Earth is a torus, with its charged particles aligned to the north-south axis. There is also a torus located in the center or heart of Mother Earth.
- **Sacred sites and crop formations:** Megalithic sites such as Avebury in the south of England are surrounded by a moat. This

doughnut- or tubelike structure and the spiraling shape created by the stones form a torus designed to focus and transform archetypal energies that enter the site during specific astronomical events. This energy is then sent out through the grid system of the Earth to affect humanity's consciousness.

- **A rainbow:** A rainbow blends seven different frequencies of light within a bow. This natural torus, often linked to a magical pot of gold at its end, reminds us of our perpetual and eternal connection to the Great Mother and the natural dance between the watery force of creation and the fire of the focused mind.
- **The sun:** Its energy field is toroidal.
- **The Galactic Center:** The Galactic Center is a toroidal-shaped black hole.
- **Great Mother:** The heart of the Great Mother is located at the Central Sun of the Central Sun and is toroidal.
- **Every human heart:** Every human heart is toroidal so that our hearts can connect, even when our minds fail to listen.

FEATURES OF THE TORUS

As our research deepens into the nature of the torus, we find it has a number of unique features:

1. It is a transformer encoded with the blueprint for creation and evolution on this planet.
2. Acting as a transformer, it is the toroidal heart that turns spirit into matter and then converts matter back into the essential nature of spirit, until immortality is achieved.
3. Once energy is generated and set in motion, the torus is self-perpetuating; in other words, it maintains its own momentum.
4. The flow is kept in constant motion by a healthy balance between equal forces of attraction and repulsion, for these two forces must work together.
5. This reminds us that our true heart accepts all parts of the self

equally without judgment or favor—seeing dark and light as equally acceptable; the result is a torus.

6. The flow within the torus is bidirectional. It enters and leaves at the top and the bottom, reminding us that spirit and matter, heaven and earth, are equally valuable and interdependent. This reflects the ancient maxim "As below, so above; as above, so below."

7. At the center of a torus is a wormhole through which our soul can pass into the multidimensional realms of unlimited potential, in other words, into the vastness of the Great Mother.

HEARTFELT COMMUNICATION

One of the most common images of a toroid is that of a doughnut-shaped ring whose surface consists of seven distinct colors. All of these colors are in touch with each other and appear to be able to communicate with each other despite their different frequencies.

From this we can surmise that when we are living from our hearts and not our heads, communication between us becomes more honest, open, and loving. This is particularly true when we fully embrace within our hearts the most unlovable parts of ourselves so that, like the Virgin dressed in white, we have nothing to hide.

Could this be the impulse behind the ability to speak in tongues? Could it be that when we listen through our hearts, we can understand each other without the need for words? Could this be the force that inspires true telepathic communication?

In James Twyman's book *Emissary of Love*[4] he questions some of the crystal children about their highly developed psychic abilities. In unison they say that such gifts are only the by-products of the power of love. They remind us that when we have no need for secrets, and shame has been transmuted into love, then we too will achieve the feat of instant communication. Such communication will not only occur between each other but it will also be possible to communicate anywhere throughout the universe, where time and space do not exist.

Can you appreciate the perfect communication that is already taking place because of the toroidal patterning of your heart, a cell, and the center of the galaxy, each programmed by the same perception of oneness? This is why joy is so important to us, as it links us to all life forms that resonate with the heart of the Great Mother.

It is probable that the Romans were unaware of the amazing potential available to them through their perpetual fire. Otherwise I do not believe they would have allowed their fire to become extinguished, possibly contributing to their downfall.

But we have the choice to keep our fire alight by continually feeding it with gems of wisdom, experiencing joy on a daily basis, and stepping beyond the need for secrets and into the pure light of our miraculous heart.

21

MAGICIAN—AQUARIUS
The Magician's Wand

Aquarius

Alchemy: distillation and coagulation
Polarity: masculine; the magician
Moon Phase: balsamic; to distill and transform

Known as *the water carrier,* the astrological sign of Aquarius is an air sign, signifying the final distillation of the light of consciousness from the transformation that takes place in the heart. Here the magician has been patiently waiting while we work to increase each strand of his wand through repeatedly cleansing old stories, distilling only the pure essence of truth and light.

DETACHED WISDOM OF AQUARIUS

As we move toward the Age of Aquarius we are going to become more familiar with the qualities of Aquarius, probably one of the most enigmatic of all the signs. The glyph of Aquarius shows a man carrying his watery emotions in a jar. This is a perfect metaphor for those with strong Aquarian tendencies who tend to avoid emotional attachments and may indeed appear cold, detached, and unfeeling. Try to emotionally blackmail an Aquarian and you'll probably hear, "There's the door, don't make a noise as you leave." With my moon in Aquarius, I once upset someone by saying, "I don't mind if you stay or leave," offering her the choice to make her own decision without any attachment, on my part, to her decision. I was met with indignation and tears as she told me that I was uncaring. That's Aquarius! We may seem cool, but in truth, we're just not interested in sticky emotional relationships, especially if they distract us from experiencing the clarity and insight found at the third eye.

Those with strong Aquarian energies have the ability see the larger picture and are never happier than when they can synthesize and understand the information they receive and then explain it to others. Their frustration comes when they are met with blank stares and realize that they may as well be talking another language. At this point they often detach, preferring their own company, especially when it includes metaphysical or unusual studies. But an Aquarian should never give in, with their wealth of knowledge their challenge is to find ways to translate and convey this information in bite-size amounts and then not become attached to the result of their efforts.

CLAIMING OUR MAGICIAN'S WAND

It is with the clarity and wisdom of the Aquarian that we are now ready to bring together the two strands of our wand that we have been carefully crafting throughout our journey. Let's look at these two strands:

- The ida was formed through the nurturing of our dreams until they transformed into matter. This took place as we moved along the ascending pathway between base and crown chakras. Here we built our ego, empowered our hero, mastered the four elements, and finally saw the hero crowned king.
- The pingala was created when form or matter dissolved back into the nebulous state of spirit. The journey we took was the descending pathway between crown and base chakras as the lover and sage journeyed into the underworld and recalled and integrated all parts of the soul back into the heart, filling the heart with rich gems of wisdom in the name of love.

The next step is for the distilled energies of the pingala to rise up and come face to face with the energies of the ida in the ajna or third eye. As the head of the manifested serpent and the head of the spiritualized serpent face each other in the shape of the infinity sign, they become the fully formed Djed or winged serpent, represented by the caduceus. We are now free to fly beyond the confines of our mind into mystery.

Figure 21.1. The staff of Hermes,
otherwise known as the *caduceus*

Through this union of spirit and matter, the third strand of the wand, the sushumna, is manifest. This trinity, acting as the magician's wand, evokes the emergence of the magician within all of us, allowing us to move with ease between the multiple dimensions of reality with just one shake of our wand.

The final step is for this winged serpent to fly upward to the crown chakra and pineal gland, magnetically attracting the Ba or divine spark to dive down to fertilize the Djed. This leads to the instantaneous release of amrita, which fully illuminates the Ka, and immortality is achieved.

At this point, there are no more questions to ponder, so let's end with a meditation to bring everything together.

As always make sure you are in a quiet and safe place where you are able to close your eyes; you may sit or lie down for this meditation.

Take a few deep breaths where the out-breath is longer than the in-breath, sending all your thoughts through your body into the ground. Now move your awareness to your heart chakra—center of your chest—and connect to your soul as it holds the blueprint of your life here on Earth.

Moving your awareness now to your feet, once again become aware of magnets on the soles of your feet and that there is an even larger magnet in Mother Earth. Surrendering to her love, allow yourself to sink into the Earth, developing roots from the soles of your feet that go in all directions. Allow the moist and nurturing soil of Mother Earth to surround and nourish your roots. When you are ready, move your awareness to the end of one of your deepest roots, the root chakra. Through this runs the golden serpentine energy of consciousness carrying all your dreams and ideas.

Tapping into your heart chakra again, gently draw golden serpentine energy up along your roots and then around your legs until it reaches your base chakra. From here, allow it to gently spiral up along the spine through each of the chakras in turn until, showering out of the top of your head, you are wearing a golden crown. Now watch as this golden energy divides into two separate energies. The left-hand serpent glides down to wait on the left-hand side of your third eye, while the serpent on the right-hand side repeatedly spirals up and down through all the chakras, shaking off any excess energy that no longer resonates with your soul.

At the completion of the process, both serpents face each other at the level of the third eye. As they unite you feel a rush of energy flowing up your spine and you feel the presence of wings that lift you free of your body and out into the starry skies.

Enjoy the freedom as long as you like before returning to Earth and then to the room where you are seated or lying. When you are ready open your eyes.

Never before has there been such a rich opportunity for each of us to reach our own perfected state as a divine being. Yet as we move toward the age of Aquarius—the age of common unity and collective responsibility—our journey is not for us alone but for all humanity. Each of us is unique; each carries a specific part of the jigsaw puzzle that must be laid in place for all of us to know unity consciousness. It is time to fulfill our destiny through self-accountability and express our soul's vibration here on Earth.

Claim your wings, soar free, and playfully glide in the currents of the Great Mother's love; she is calling you. What a wonderful time to be alive!

CONCLUSION

EMBRACED BY
THE GREAT MOTHER

I hope you've enjoyed the insights held within this book as much as I have benefited from receiving them and sharing them with you. I'd like to share a final meditation that aptly sums up my respect and love for the Great Mother.

The perspiration is running down my back in tiny rivers as I sit in the darkness, entranced by the rhythmic tones of the drums. I'm in a sweat lodge, or *inipi,* following one of the most sacred ceremonies of the Native American tradition. A low dome-shaped structure built from natural materials, the lodge is believed to represent the womb of the Great Mother, offering new beginnings and insights to those who enter with reverence and humility.

Inside the inipi it is dark, apart from the glow emanating from the rocks, or "grandfathers," that have been placed with great care and attention in the central pit. These spirits of the stone kingdom have been selected specifically by the medicine man who is leading our ceremony; he respects their wisdom and ability to inspire our prayers and meditations. As water is poured onto the stones, the temperature in the lodge increases and I'm instantly enveloped by the breath of these great beings and urged to focus my awareness more deeply inward.

Now it's time to speak my prayers aloud, allowing the smoke and steam to carry them beyond the inipi to Wakan Takan, the Great Spirit. As I come to the end of my appreciation for those who had lived upon the Earth and those who have passed into the world of spirit, I find myself sending loving thoughts to the star people. This surprises me because, although I respect my extraterrestrial connections, they do not usually feature in my prayers.

Such association with the star people extends back to my early childhood, when a tunnel of light would lightly touch the top of my head as I lay in my cradle at night. I felt no fear. Rather, I sensed the opening of a portal to a world I knew beyond this Earth plane. With joy, I would find myself entering the tunnel and merging immediately with a field of energy—a kind of journey that felt like coming home.

When I was old enough to tell my mother about these nightly visits, she said wisely, "I don't know where you are going, but if you feel joy, follow your heart and you will find your path." It was many years later that a medium helped me to understand these energetic travels: "You do know you come from the stars?" At that moment, for the first time in my life, I felt I'd been seen, with my heart knowing what my head had struggled to understand.

Since then my connection to the star people has remained constant, with no need for greater explanation. Yet here I am in the inipi sending prayers out into the galaxy, and I am amazed to hear the medicine man saying soon after: "There is a very old spirit from the stars who wants to join this ceremony. I will welcome him with song—and then hold on to your hats; we're going on a celestial journey!"

With that more heated stones are added to the pit, the door is closed, and the songs begin. Immediately, I find myself moving rapidly skyward accompanied by two dolphins, whom I consider interdimensional travelers. As we leave the Earth's atmosphere, I look back and am surprised to see a vibrant mass of brilliant blue energy emanating from the planet's surface. This is unlike any pictures taken by astronauts; I know I am viewing the energetic aura of Gaia.

Our journey upward ends in front of a long table with nine chairs.

Eight are positioned on either side of the table, facing each other, and one is placed at the head of the table. It is clear I am to sit in this seat. As I do, from beneath my feet to above my head, I am immediately flooded with all the energy from the other eight positions around the table until my body is electric. In this moment I know I have entered and embodied the ninth dimension associated with the Great Mother. My heart is resonating with her heart, around which billions of stars and planets are orbiting in perfect harmony.

Through my heart, I hear a voice speak to me: "I am the heart of the Great Mother, the perpetual fire of the galaxy. I am toroidal in shape, and it is through me that the consciousness of every star, planet, and life-form achieves transformation. It is through me that the essential energy of spirit passes into matter and matter transforms eventually back into my ocean of unlimited possibilities. Each star you see in the galaxy is the heart of a solar system, communicating instantaneously with the heart of every living being on the planets orbiting the star. All is connected with the initial pulse or frequency set by the heart at the center of each galaxy.

"Inherent in all human beings is a signature frequency specific to a particular star and galaxy. This frequency is carried within their skin color, language, songs, physical shape, and even in the way they connect to the land. In the same way, the nature kingdoms resonate with the stars through their shapes, colors, and sounds. Unfortunately, over time, humanity has become disconnected, not only from the natural world but also from the built-in signal calling them to remember their multidimensional origins. Yet on a clear starlit night, it is not uncommon to find yourself looking out at the stars and wondering why certain constellations seem to attract your attention.

"The great shift in consciousness occurring on planet Earth at this time is not exclusive to you. Many celestial bodies are experiencing change and are calling on their children here on Earth to remember who they are and open their hearts to their star family. But I offer a note of clarification: It's not enough to believe or even know you come from the stars. To know your celestial self it is essential to continue your inner work, strengthening your Ka or light body until you are light enough to fly between the worlds."

I know my time with the Great Mother is coming to a close, and thus I ask her a question: "What words of advice do you offer to us so we can make the most of the great changes that lie ahead?"

Through my heart, I hear the answer: "Still your mind and become centered in your heart. As Mother Earth is also transforming into her perfect light body, it is important to keep a firm connection with her so you can easily surf the waves of change. Then, connecting first to the torus within your own heart, root yourself into Mother Earth as you have been taught. Pass beyond the root chakra and into the very center or heart of Mother Earth, pass through this torus and swiftly toward the toroidal portal of your sun. Recognizing this gateway as an interdimensional golden disc, pass through it with the innocence of a child and progress to the heart of the Galactic Mother. As you move through this wormhole with humility and gratitude, allow your awareness to eventually merge with the energies at the heart of the Central Sun of the Central Sun—the Great Mother. You are home. Remember as hearts connect there is only 'Now' and within the Now there is only love—for that is the elixir of life."

And with that I find myself journeying swiftly back toward the Earth until I feel the cool ground under my body and I'm wrapped in the intense darkness of the inipi. The songs are ending, the ceremony is almost complete, and yet the next stage of my journey has just begun. As we step out into the cool night air, we look up to see the Milky Way snaking its way across the sky above. My heart reaches out to all children of the stars with the hope that each will hear the call of the Great Mother and know the embrace of her unbounded love.

NOTES

INTRODUCTION
TEACHINGS BENEATH THE STARS

1. Barrios, *The Book of Destiny,* 121.
2. Henry, *Oracle of the Illuminati,* 188–90.
3. Barrios, *The Book of Destiny,* 130.
4. Barrios, *The Book of Destiny,* 124.
5. Jenkins, *Maya Cosmogenesis 2012,* 31.
6. Jenkins, *Maya Cosmogenesis 2012,* 52.
7. Jenkins, *Maya Cosmogenesis 2012,* 25.
8. Kaku, *Hyperspace,* 16.
9. Comings, "Essential Nature of Space."
10. Hauk, *Emerald Tablet,* 45.
11. Kenyon and Sion, *Magdalen Manuscript,* 115–31.
12. Prophet and Clare Prophet, *St. Germain on Alchemy,* 12.
13. Tedlock, *Popul Vuh.*
14. Robinson, ed., *Nag Hammadi Library in English,* 131; The Gospel of Thomas, verse 39.

1. THE TRIPLE GODDESS

1. Ensler, *Vagina Monologues.*
2. Knud Mariboe, "Denmark," The Encyclopædia of the Celts (website, no longer available).
3. Jones, *Ancient British Goddess,* 125.

4. Murphy, "About the Iroquois Constitution."

4. THE CRONE

1. Jones, *Ancient British Goddess,* 125.
2. Kenyon and Sion, *Magdalen Manuscript,* 20.

6. THE ALCHEMICAL EMERALD TABLET

1. Prophet and Prophet, *St. Germain on Alchemy,* 6.
2. Doreal, *Emerald Tablets of Thoth.*
3. Hauk, *Emerald Tablet,* 22.
4. Hauk, *Emerald Tablet,* 25–30.
5. Ahmed, *Moses and Akhenaten.*
6. Hauk, *Emerald Tablet,* 3.
7. Hauk, *Emerald Tablet,* 45.
8. Hauk, *Emerald Tablet,* 165.

7. RHYTHMS OF THE MOON

1. Rudhyar, *Lunation Cycle.*
2. George, *Finding Our Way,* 15.
3. George, *Finding Our Way,* 16–39.

8. THE GREAT MOTHER'S CELESTIAL ALCHEMY

1. Jenkins, *Maya Cosmogenesis 2012,* 205.
2. Spiller, *Astrology for the Soul,* 9–17.

11. BOY-CHILD—ARIES

1. Bailey, *Esoteric Healing,* 183–87.

13. HERO—GEMINI

1. Campbell, *Hero with a Thousand Faces.*

14. CRONE—CANCER

1. Wolkstein and Kramer, *Inanna,* 4–9.

16. VIRGIN/TRIPLE GODDESS—VIRGO

1. Wolkstein and Kramer, *Inanna,* 52–57.

18. CRONE/TRIPLE GODDESS—SCORPIO

1. Wolkstein and Kramer, *Inanna*, 52–60.
2. Wolkstein and Kramer, *Inanna*, 62–67.
3. Nhat Hanh, *Please Call Me by My True Names*, 72.

20. TRIPLE GODDESS—CAPRICORN

1. Pinkham, *Return of the Serpents of Wisdom*, Loc 982 of 7694.
2. Khan, *Teachings of Hazrat Inayat Khan*, vol. 1, chapter 8.
3. Pearce, *Biology of Transcendence*, 57.
4. Twyman, *Emissary of Love*, 48.

BIBLIOGRAPHY

Ahmed, Osman. *Moses and Akhenaten: The Secret History of Egypt at the Time of the Exodus.* Rochester, Vt.: Bear & Co., 2002.

Bailey, Alice. *Esoteric Astrology.* London: Lucis Press Ltd., 1951.

———. *Esoteric Healing.* London: Lucis Press Ltd., 1953.

Barrios, Carlos. *Kam Wuj, El Libro del Destino* (The Book of Destiny). Buenos Aires: South American Editorial, 2000.

Campbell, Joseph. *The Hero with a Thousand Faces.* New York: Bollingen Foundation, 1949.

Comings, Mark. "The Essential Nature of Space, Time, and Light Consciousness." Paper presented at the International Institute of Integral Human Sciences Conference. Montreal, 2005.

Doreal, M. *Hermes Trismegiste.* Paris: Messrs. Firmin Didot, 1858.

———. *The Emerald Tablets of Thoth, the Atlantean.* Nashville, Tenn.: Source Books and Sacred Spaces, 1996.

Ensler, Eve. *The Vagina Monologues.* New York: Random House, 1998.

Gardner, Laurence. *Genesis and the Grail Kings.* Gloucester, Mass.: Fair Wind Press, 2002.

George, Demetra. *Finding Our Way through the Dark.* San Diego: ACS Publications, 1994.

Hauk, Dennis William. *The Emerald Tablet.* New York: Penguin Books, 1999.

Henry, William. *Oracle of the Illuminati.* Kempton, Ill.: Adventures Unlimited Press, 2005.

Jenkins, John Major. *Maya Cosmogenesis 2012.* Rochester, Vt.: Bear & Co., 1998.

Jones, Kathy. *The Ancient British Goddess*. Glastonbury, UK: Ariadne Publications, 2001.

Jung, C. G. *Psychology and Alchemy*. New York: Bollingen Foundation, 1968.

Kaku, Michio. *Hyperspace*. New York: Anchor Books, 1994.

Kelley, David H. "Mesoamerican Astronomy and the Maya Calendar Correlation Problem," *Memorias del Segundo Coloquio Internacional de Mayistas* 1 (1989).

Kenyon, Tom, and Judi Sion. *The Magdalen Manuscript*. Orcas, Wash.: ORB Communications, 2002.

Khan, Hazrat Inayat. *Teachings of Hazrat Inayat Khan; Purpose of life*. Wahiduddin's Web: Living from the Heart (website), vol. 1, chapter 8.

Kinstler, Clysta. *The Moon under Her Feet*. San Francisco: HarperCollins, 1991.

Knight, Christopher, and Robert Lomas. *The Hiram Key*. London: Element Books, 1997.

Möller, Lennart. *The Exodus Case: New Discoveries Confirm the Historical Exodus*. Copenhagen: Scandinavia Publishing House, 2000.

Murphy, Gerald. "About the Iroquois Constitution." In "Modern History Sourcebook: The Constitution of the Iroquois Confederacy," Fordham University (website).

Nhat Hanh, Thich. *Please Call Me by My True Names*. Berkeley: Parallel Press, 1999.

Pearce, Joseph Chilton. *The Biology of Transcendence*. Rochester, Vt.: Park Street Press, 2002.

Pinkham, Mark Amaru. *Return of the Serpents of Wisdom*. Kempton, Ill.: Adventures Unlimited Press, 2015.

Prophet, Mark, and Elizabeth Clare Prophet. *St. Germain on Alchemy*. Corwin Springs, Mont.: Summit University Press, 1993.

Robinson, James, ed. *The Nag Hammadi Library in English*. San Francisco: HarperCollins, 1990.

Rudhyar, Dane. *The Lunation Cycle*. Santa Fe: Aurora Press, 1978.

Sitchin, Zecharia. *The 12th Planet*. Rochester, Vt.: Bear & Co., 1991.

Spiller, Jan. *Astrology for the Soul*. New York: Bantam Books, 1997.

Spretnak, Charlene. *Lost Goddesses of Early Greece: A Collection of Pre-Hellenic Myths*. Boston: Beacon Press, 1981.

Tedlock, Dennis. *The Popul Vuh: The Definitive Edition of the Mayan Book of the Dawn of Life and the Glories of the Gods and Kings.* New York: Simon and Schuster, 1996.

Twyman, James. *Emissary of Love.* Findhorn, UK: Findhorn Press, 2002.

Walker, Barbara. *The Woman's Encyclopedia of Myths and Secrets.* San Francisco: Harper, 1983.

Wolkstein, Diane, and Samuel Noah Kramer. *Inanna, Queen of Heaven and Earth.* New York: Harper, 1983.

INDEX

Page numbers in *italics* indicate illustrations

BOOKS OF RELATED INTEREST

The Healing Power of the Sacred Woman
Health, Creativity, and Fertility for the Soul
by Christine R. Page, M.D.

The Triple Goddess Tarot
The Power of the Major Arcana, Chakra Healing,
and the Divine Feminine
by Isha Lerner
Illustrated by Mara Friedman
Foreword by Vicki Noble

Awakening the Ancient Power of Snake
Transformation, Healing, and Enlightenment
by Dawn Baumann Brunke

Fierce Feminine Rising
Heal from Predatory Relationships and Recenter Your Personal Power
by Anaiya Sophia

Healing Journeys with the Black Madonna
Chants, Music, and Sacred Practices of the Great Goddess
by Alessandra Belloni
Foreword by Matthew Fox

Womb Awakening
Initiatory Wisdom from the Creatrix of All Life
by Azra Bertrand, M.D., and Seren Bertrand

Return of the Divine Sophia
Healing the Earth through the Lost Wisdom Teachings
of Jesus, Isis, and Mary Magdalene
by Tricia McCannon

The Gospel of Mary Magdalene
by Jean-Yves Leloup
Foreword by Jacob Needleman

INNER TRADITIONS • BEAR & COMPANY
P.O. Box 388, Rochester, VT 05767
1-800-246-8648 • www.InnerTraditions.com

Or contact your local bookseller